TEACHING SOCIAL STUDIES
TO THE YOUNG CHILD

SOURCE BOOKS ON EDUCATION
(VOL. 29)

GARLAND REFERENCE LIBRARY
OF SOCIAL SCIENCE
(VOL. 457)

SOURCE BOOKS ON EDUCATION

TEACHING SOCIAL STUDIES
TO THE YOUNG CHILD
A Research and Resource Guide

Blythe S. Farb Hinitz

GARLAND PUBLISHING, INC. • NEW YORK & LONDON
1992

Library of Congress Cataloging-in-Publication Data

Hinitz, Blythe Simone Farb, 1944–
    Teaching social studies to the young child : a research and
resource guide / Blythe S. Farb Hinitz.
        p.   cm. — (Garland reference library of social science ; vol.
457. Source books on education ; vol. 29.)
    Includes bibliographical references and index.
    ISBN 0-8240-4439-8
    1. Social sciences—Study and teaching (Early childhood)—United
States. I. Title. II. Series: Garland reference library of social
science ; vol. 457. III. Series: Garland reference library of
social science. Source books on education ; vol. 29.
LB1139.5.S64H56   1992
372.83'044'0973—dc20   91-28885
                                                                 CIP

Printed on acid-free, 250-year-life paper
Manufactured in the United States of America

Dedicated
to my father

Max S. Farb (1908–1988)

who showed me the sundial in the
Brooklyn Botanic Gardens and
told me to reach for the sky.

With appreciation and thanks to
my husband
Dr. Herman J. Hinitz
for his unfailing support through the years.

My parents, Gertrude A. and Max S. Farb,
my first social studies teachers.

My family.

CONTENTS

ACKNOWLEDGMENTS

My sincere appreciation to the entire staff of the Roscow L. West Library at Trenton State College, and especially to Janice Kisthardt, Carol Miklovis, Fred Chin, and Pat Beaber, for demonstrating that library science is an art.

My grateful appreciation and sincere thanks to the Dean of the School of Education, Dr. Philip A. Ollio, and to the members of the Departments of Elementary and Early Childhood Education and Reading and Language Arts for their support.

To Dr. Carol Seefeldt, University of Maryland, College Park, thank you for opening the door to research in early childhood social studies.

Many individuals have authored or referenced publications which broadened and enhanced this work. In particular, I would like to thank Lesley Abbott of the Faculty of Community Studies and Education, Didsbury School of Education, Manchester Polytechnic, United Kingdom; Dr. Elliott Seif, Curriculum and Instruction, Bucks County Intermediate Unit, Pennsylvania; Dr. Dick Puglisi, University of South Florida, Tampa; Dr. Saul Barr, University of Tennessee, Martin; Dr. Lynn Liben, Dr. Roger Downs, and Debra Daggs, Pennsylvania State University; Dr. Robert Stout, New Jersey Council on Economic Education; and Dr. Linda Levstik, University of Kentucky, for their cooperation in providing research materials.

I would like to express my gratitude to the following publishers who provided materials for review:

Afton Publishing Company
Addison Wesley
Allyn and Bacon, Inc.
Charles Merrill
D.C. Heath
Harper & Row, Publishers
Holt Rinehart and Winston
Houghton Mifflin Company
Longman
Macmillan/McGraw Hill
Modern Curriculum Press
Oryx Press
Prentice Hall
Random House
Scott Foresman/Goodyear
Silver Burdett and Ginn
Teachers College Press

To my family, friends and colleagues who have offered their suggestions and provided assistance during the preparation of this book, thank you.

All errors and omissions are the responsibility of the author. Comments, reports of omission, and information regarding the availability of new studies and publications for inclusion in future supplements to this book should be sent to the author.

PREFACE

This volume was written to provide references to resources and research in the field of early childhood social studies education. The book contains essays and annotations on selected areas of early childhood social studies education. The first section of the book includes chapters about geography, economics and history education for young children. Chapters dealing with teacher education texts in the fields of early childhood and elementary social studies, and student texts and teacher's manuals for grades kindergarten to three comprise the second section of the book. A summary chapter detailing current and future issues in the field concludes the volume.

The author defines early childhood education programs as traditional and non-traditional programs for children between the ages of three and eight years, in public and non-public educational settings. These include, but are not limited to, nursery school, day care, kindergarten, and primary level settings. An early childhood educator is viewed as a person who cares for and guides young children and/or their teachers in all areas of development.

Some of the social science disciplines and social studies areas subsumed under the heading of early childhood social studies are: economics, geography, history, multicultural and peace education, psychology, sociology, anthropology, law-related education, and affective and values education. The disciplines of geography, economics and history have been selected for inclusion in this volume for two reasons. Concepts from these disciplines have become an integral part of the early childhood curriculum, and authors have provided written guidance about how each discipline fits into the social studies, for both the classroom teacher and the researcher. Other authors have written appropriate resource and research volumes for some of the areas mentioned above. Examples of such publications are detailed below.

There are many available resources on the topic of multicultural education. *Multicultural Education: A Source Book* by Patricia G. Ramsey, Edwina Battle Vold, and Leslie R. Williams provides an excellent overview of the evolution of multicultural education, curricula and strategies, teacher education, and future directions. The following books deal specifically with multicultural education for young children: *Anti-Bias Curriculum: Tools for Empowering Young Children* by Louise Derman-Sparks and the A.B.C. Task Force, *Diversity in the Classroom: A Multicultural Approach to the Education of Young Children* by Frances E. Kendall, *Teaching and Learning in a Diverse World: Multicultural Education for Young Children* by Patricia G. Ramsey, *Understanding the Multicultural Experience in Early Childhood Education* edited by Olivia N. Saracho and Bernard Spodek, and *Early Childhood Bilingual Education: A Hispanic Perspective* edited by Theresa Herrera Escobedo. The area of peace education in early childhood will be addressed in the forthcoming third edition of *Resources for Early Childhood: An Annotated Bibliography and Guide for Educators, Librarians, Health Care Professionals, and Parents* edited by Hannah Nuba. An existing curriculum resource is: *Educating for Global Responsibility: Teacher-Designed Curricula for Peace Education, K–12* edited by Betty A. Reardon.

Available research in psychology, sociology and anthropology is summarized by Nelson and Stahl in their chapter in the *Handbook of Research on Social Studies Teaching and Learning* (Shaver, 1991). Patrick and Hoge discuss the teaching of government, civics, and law in the same volume. Schuncke and Krough (1985) and Nelson (1980) have written about the area of law-related education and young children. Affective processes and aims are the subject of Scott's chapter in Shaver (1991).

REFERENCES

Derman-Sparks, L. (1989). *Anti-bias curriculum: Tools for empowering young children.* Washington, D.C.: National Association for the Education of Young Children.

Escobedo, T.H. (Ed.). (1983). *Early childhood bilingual education: A Hispanic perspective.* New York: Teachers College Press.

Hinitz, B.F. (forthcoming). Peace education for young children. In H. Nuba (Ed.). *Resources for early childhood: An annotated bibliography and guide for educators, librarians, health care professionals, and parents.* (3rd ed.). Garland Publishing, Inc.

Kendall, F.E. (1983). *Diversity in the classroom: A multicultural approach to the education of young children.* New York: Teachers College Press.

Nelson, M.R. (1980, April/May). Teaching young children about the law. *Childhood Education, 56*(5), 274–277.

———, M.R., & Stahl, R.J. (1991). Teaching anthropology, sociology, and psychology. In J.P. Shaver (Ed.). *Handbook of research on social studies teaching and learning: A project of the National Council for the Social Studies.* (pp. 420–426). New York: Macmillan Publishing Company.

Patrick, J.J., & Hoge, J.D. (1991). Teaching government, civics, and law. In J.P. Shaver (Ed.). *Handbook of research on social studies teaching and learning: A project of the National Council for the Social Studies.* (pp. 427–436). New York: Macmillan Publishing Company.

Ramsey, P.G. (1987). *Teaching and learning in a diverse world: Multicultural education for young children.* New York: Teachers College Press.

———, Vold, E.B., & Williams, L.R. (1989). *Multicultural education: A source book.* New York: Garland Publishing, Inc.

Reardon, B.A. (Ed.). (1988). *Educating for global responsibility: Teacher-designed curricula for peace education, K–12.* New York: Teachers College Press.

Saracho, O.N., & Spodek, B. (1983). *Understanding the multicultural experience in early childhood education.* Washington, D.C.: National Association for the Education of Young Children.

Schuncke, G.M., & Krogh, S.L. (1985, May/June). Law-related education and the young child. *The Social Studies 76*(3), 139–142.

Scott, K.P. (1991). Achieving social studies affective aims: Values, empathy, and moral development. In J.P. Shaver (Ed.). *Handbook of research on social studies teaching and learning: A project of the National Council for the Social Studies.* (pp. 357–369). New York: Macmillan Publishing Company.

Shaver, J.P. (Ed.). (1991). *Handbook of research on social studies teaching and learning: A project of the National Council for the Social Studies.* New York: Macmillan Publishing Company.

Wyner, N.B., & Farquhar, E. (1991). Cognitive, emotional, and social development: Early childhood social studies. In J.P. Shaver (Ed.). *Handbook of research on social studies teaching and learning: A project of the National Council for the Social Studies.* (pp. 109–120). New York: Macmillan Publishing Company.

TEACHING SOCIAL STUDIES TO THE YOUNG CHILD

School children studying a map. Photo by Arthur Rothstein, Greenbelt, Maryland, April, 1939. Library of Congress.

Chapter 1

GEOGRAPHY

A clogged rain gutter, and other structural problems, causes the roof of a Texas department store to collapse under the weight of a heavy rainfall, killing close to fifty people. The farm belt broils under summer temperatures which daily exceed one hundred degrees, but some farmers in Nebraska have water for irrigation. They can draw on the water of an underground river which runs through a portion of the midwest. These examples related to natural phenomena graphically depict the necessity for the use of geographic understandings in everyday life. How can we define the "mother of sciences" (Pattison, 1964) in order to develop a clearer understanding of its important role in our lives? Gritzner (1985) views geography as involving the study of "WHAT (physical and human features of the earth's surfaces), WHERE (locational data), WHY (explanation of processes or causative agents), and WHAT OF IT (significance)." Long ago Lucy Sprague Mitchell (1934) defined it as consisting of facts (locational and physical geography) and relationships (human geography). Pagano (1978) defined it from the child's viewpoint as "the environment in which I live." Stoltman (1991) says geography is recognized as the spatial science concerned with the location of elements on the earth's surface and their relationship to each other.

Human beings begin their development of geographic concepts as infants and toddlers (Catling, 1978; Hewes, 1982; Sunal & Sunal, 1978). According to Blaut and Stea, cross-cultural and developmental research on the untaught mapping abilities of children five through ten suggests that mapping behavior is a normal and important process in human development and that map learning begins long before the child encounters formal geography and cartography (1971).

Rice and Cobb cite numerous studies in support of their arguments that the map abilities which children possess prior to instruction have not been appropriately assessed by conventional means, and that it is not necessary to wait until grade four or five to introduce systematic conceptual learning and skills related to geography (1979).

Geography has been a part of the elementary school curriculum since the seventeenth century. "Public responsiveness to the importance of geography as a school subject developed after 1830 (when) . . . a number of states passed laws requiring the teaching of geography and the study of the geography of the home state" (Stoltman, 1986). The work of such Europeans as Pestalozzi and Guyot, and of Harvard professor William Morris Davis led to several practices which remain important to the present day. Pestalozzi's belief that direct observation and sense perception are essential to meaningful learning led to the study of the home region through direct observation, and to the introduction of map drawing and experiments using globes into the curriculum. The influence of Morris, in the 1800s, led to a change in the instructional methods in physical geography from recitation of factual information to the study of geography as an earth science (Stoltman, 1986).

According to Muessig (1987), elementary geographic education has always been plagued by low-level, fragmented content. Typical past approaches have often tried the patience, killed the interest, stifled the imagination, and insulted the intelligence of learners. There have been some bright spots, however. In the writings of the period 1900–1919, the idea that children should be taught to think geographically emerged. In the '20s and '30s, the major stated objective of geography teaching was "training for American citizenship and for broad-minded, noble citizenship in the world" (Muessig, 1987). The book *Young Geographers* (Mitchell, 1934), a milestone in natural methods of instruction, was published during this time period. The major work of the period 1940–1959 was *The Teaching of Geography* by Zoe Thralls, who had published an earlier chapter, "Geography in the Elementary School," in the 32nd Yearbook of the National Society for the Study of Education (Whipple, 1933). In that chapter, Thralls stated that work in the primary grades was integrated, and therefore had no strict subject-matter divisions. She defined the chief objective of the primary school as, "to develop skill in the use of the fundamental tools of learning; namely, ability to read, write, and use numbers in simple computation" (1933). Thralls encouraged the use of interesting concrete experiences with the children's own environment. Reeder, in the same volume, identified manipulation of real things, activity as a method of thinking, and providing for learnings that have meaning for the child, as underlying principles of "modern method" (1933). In a later work, Scarfe re-emphasized many of these points, stating that, "the learning of valuable geographical concepts is subsidiary at this age to the development of fundamental skills" (1965). He included experiences out-of-doors, study of local geographical material, field trips, and stories of far-away countries, in a proposed geography readiness program for children six to nine years of age.

The ferment in social studies education during the '60s and '70s was readily apparent in the field of geography. The Georgia Geography Curriculum Project of the 1970s provided a nucleus of research. The 33rd Yearbook of the National Council for the Social Studies (1963) contained a chapter on "Developing a Sense of Place and Space" by Lorrin Kennamer. In addition to noting the contribution of geography to social studies, the chapter discussed the functions of maps, and basic map and globe skills. This publication, and the *Curriculum Guide for Geographic Education* (Hill, 1964) of the National Council for Geographic Education, became mainstays of primary geography curricula until they were superseded by the publication of the *Guidelines for Geographic Education* (AAG-NCGE, 1984), which proposes five central themes to be used in geographic inquiry, and *K-6 Geography: Themes, Key Ideas, and Learning Opportunities* (GENIP, 1987). The five themes, which have been incorporated into some current social studies curricula, are:

1. Location: Position on the Earth's Surface
2. Place: Physical and Human Characteristics
3. Relationships Within Places: Humans and Environments
4. Movement: Humans Interacting on the Earth
5. Regions: How They Form and Change

The introduction to *K-6 Geography: Themes, Key Ideas, and Learning Opportunities* sets the tone for geographic education in the nineties with the following statement:

> Geographic education at the elementary school level is based upon existing knowledge of the stages of childrens' cognitive, psychological and social development as well as key geographic understandings. The rich and varied life experiences of children should be used as much as possible to illustrate and develop the learning opportunities selected for study. Use of the learning opportunities requires that they be adapted to meet local objectives and at particular grade levels in ways which meet the needs of children with varying experiential backgrounds, and differing language and intellectual abilities. (GENIP, 1987)

Geography plays a prominant role in the method devised by Dr. Maria Montessori in the early 1900s. A major objective for the inclusion of geography was the development of spatial orientation through interaction and experience with the environment and materials. A second objective for the three to seven year old child was becoming aware of and accepting other cultures through related experiences in cultural studies. (Seldin & Raymond, 1981; [Kocher, 1972]). Lucy Sprague Mitchell (1934) differentiated dictated materials from adaptable materials. For Mitchell, Montessori materials, picture books, models to copy, reciting verses, and using textbooks are examples of activities dictated by the teacher. Carolyn Pratt unit blocks, crayons and paper, clay, playing with language, and source materials relevant to the situation, are examples of placing children in a position to explore and to use the environment as a laboratory. Mitchell's rationale for "a laboratory well equipped with . . . appropriate tools" is that, "content . . . is now discovered, used, related through a curriculum of experience, rather than gathered together in convenient ready-made parcels called textbooks."

Gardner, Chair of the National Commission on Excellence in Education, gives another rationale for the study of geography in the school curriculum:

> Children born in the desert lands of Nevada, or the small coves of West Virginia, or even the canyons of Manhattan have been able to look beyond their local worlds as they study the people and places of distant nations and regions. This comprehension of distinct and sometimes vividly divergent ways of life provides children with a wonderful vision of the world and their place in it. It is not only a vision of life lived differently; it is a vision that leads to a better understanding of one's own way of life. To study another place, another society, another people is always to explore one's own universe through contrast and comparison. (1986)

The literature discusses several basic traditions of geography. Among them are the spatial (choreographic), area studies (regional geography), man-land (ecological or cultural geography), earth science (physical geography), and political geography traditions (Pattison, 1964; deLeeuw, 1967). The spatial tradition deals with the location, layout and movement (distance, direction) of what is seen and mapped. Political geography deals with how the political system impresses itself on the landscape. Area studies deals with the nature of places, their character, their differentiation, and what a given place is like as a totality. The man-land tradition describes the relationship and the interaction between human beings and their environment. The earth science tradition deals with the arrangement and functioning of natural things on the surface of the earth, the atmosphere surrounding the earth, and the association between earth and sun. In surveying early childhood geography curriculum and activities publications, one can find examples of each of these traditions.

The classical concerns theme, which incorporates research by leading cognitive and developmental theorists, is exemplified by the statement of the GENIP above (Stoltman, 1979). The influential work of Bruner and of Piaget are subsumed under this theme. For example, Meyer (1973) states that Bruner's discussion of enactive, iconic, and symbolic representational systems contributes to learning by helping to explain the child's development of the ability to symbolize. Muir and Cheek (1986) detail the following sequence of related perceptual experiences:

- an enactive experience which requires concrete interaction with the concept, such as a walking tour of a familiar area
- an iconic representation which allows the child to depict or remember a concept with graphic or mental images, such as examining an aerial photograph of the same area to identify specific features
- a verbal or written symbolization that abstractly represents the concept, such as the tracing of major features of the photo onto transparent plastic which is then separated from the photo. The transparency drawing becomes a map when it is separated from the photo.

Piagetian theory plays an important role in the geography education literature of the '70s and '80s. The egocentrism of children in the sensory-motor, preoperational, and concrete operational stages is cited by many authors as the reason primary school children cannot deal with certain abstract geographical concepts. For this reason, concrete, first-hand, manipulative experiences which physically and mentally involve children with their own environment are important. Richards (1983) points out that teachers of geographic skills should try to enhance cognitive development by making use of the factors of maturation, experience, and equilibration. Blaut and Stea (1974) report that during free play, children between the ages of three and six will assemble landscape-feature toys into a map-like model of a macro-environment. Because the region represented is too large to be perceived as a whole from any one vantage point, they note the necessity for a cognitive map if the child is to demonstrate comprehension. This they relate to the simple communication model of a map, i.e. the transmission and receipt, in any medium, of information about distance, direction, and landscape features of a site (1971). From these few examples, it can be seen that map-related activities must be coordinated with the child's level or stage of cognitive development.

The approaches to teaching mapping skills can be divided into systematic or sequential and needs generated. The map skills sequence theme utilizes empirical and experimental studies to attempt to reveal an appropriate sequence for the geographic skills development of young children (Stoltman, 1979). The systematic approach demands a listing of "map skills and their prerequisite understandings, that can guide teachers through the introduction, development and maintenance of the skills through the school levels" (Hawkins, 1979). In the needs approach, map skills are introduced as they are needed to accomplish content objectives.

Thinking skills precede performance (behavioral) objectives; they are not inherited givens (Brown, 1986). Children should develop skills in observing, recognizing and collecting data, classifying, ordering, representing data, developing conceptual meaning, drawing inferences and making generalizations, and talking about relationships, prior to formal map work.

Key geography-related concepts to be learned with any approach include: location and spatial relationships (where is it?), distance (how far is it?), direction, symbolization (interpreting symbols, what is it?), scale (how big is it?), orientation, projection (how can a round earth be shown on flat paper?), perspective, representation (recognizing a globe as a model of the earth), imagining relief, understanding elevation, and territoriality. Work with map projections, use of latitude and longitude, comparison of different map scales, understanding of time zones and interpretation involving two or more maps are not appropriate for primary level students.

Map activities initially derive from body movement. During the geography readiness phase, children pass through several stages as they move from three dimensional to abstract representation. Children use three dimensional miniature models (houses, cars), followed by three dimensional non-thematic models (blocks, boxes). These are followed by two dimensional "picture maps" (Van Cleaf, 1985) using precut paper shapes or magazine pictures. Melahn (1989) suggests asking the child to draw familiar objects from a "top-down" perspective. Later the child executes "drawn maps" using crayon, marker or pencil lines. There are several sub-stages in the development of map drawing (Cobb, 1977, Stoltman, 1979). Children may then map their classroom, their school, and their neighborhood. The child may have concurrent experiences with globes depicting just land and water. Only after numerous experiences in each of these stages should children be introduced to commercially-produced maps and globes. At this point they enter the stages of map reading, which begin with simple visualization or perception of the map symbols, apperception (relating the map symbols to what they actually represent), and recognizing patterns and locations of items on a map (Stoltman, 1979).

Geography is an important part of our daily lives and of the early childhood curriculum. The publications cited on the following pages represent a cross section of classical and current thinking in the field.

REFERENCES

Allen, S. J. (1989). *Maps, charts, graphs.* Levels A, B. *The places around me, Neighborhoods.* Cleveland, OH: Modern Curriculum Press.

Blaut, J. M., & Stea, D. (1974). Mapping at the age of three. *The Journal of Geography, 73*(7), 5–9.

————. (1971). Studies of geographic learning. *Annals of the Association of American Geographers, 61,* 387–393.

Brown, R. (1986, November-December). Map, globe and graphing readiness activities: Developing universal thinking skills. *Social Studies, 77*(3), 229–233.

Catling, S. J. (1978). The child's spatial conception and geographic education. *The Journal of Geography, 71*(1), 24–28.

Cobb, R. (1977). Perspective ability and map conceptualization in elementary school children. *Journal of Social Studies Research, 1*(1), 10–19.

Daggs, D. G. (1986, May). *Children's understanding of geographic hierarchies.* Paper presented at the Sixteenth Annual Symposium of the Jean Piaget Society, Philadelphia, PA.

deLeeuw, G. [1967]. Contributions of the discipline of geography to the social studies. (ERIC Document Reproduction Service No. ED 066 380)

Dowd, F. (1990, March-April). Geography **is** children's literature, math, science, art and a whole world of activities. *Journal of Geography, 89*(2), 68–73.

Downs, R. M., & Liben, L. S. (1986). Children's understanding of maps. In P. Ellen & C. Thinus-Blanc (Eds.), *Cognitive processes and spatial orientation in animal and man. Vol. 1. Neurophysiology of spatial knowledge and developmental aspects.* Dordrecht, Holland: Martinius Nijhoff.

————. (1988). Through a map darkly: Understanding maps as representations. *The Genetic Epistemologist, 16*(1), 11–18.

———, & Daggs, D. G. (1988). On education and geographers: The role of cognitive developmental theory in geographic education. *Annals of the Association of American Geographers, 78*(4), 680–700.

Foreman, D. I., & Allen, S. J. (1990). *Maps, charts, graphs.* Levels C, D. *Communities, States and regions.* Cleveland, OH: Modern Curriculum Press.

Gardner, D. P. (1986, March). Geography in the school curriculum. *Annals of the Association of American Geographers, 76* (1), 1–4.

Gerhardt, L. (1973). *Moving and knowing: The child orients himself in space.* Englewood Cliffs, NJ: Prentice Hall.

Geographic Education National Implementation Project (GENIP). (1987). *K-6 geography: Themes, key ideas, and learning opportunities.* Macomb, IL National Council for Geographic Education.

Gritzner, C. F. (1984–1985). Geography's role in the back-to-basics movement. *The Social Studies Teacher, VI,* pp. 1 and 5.

Haas, M. E. & Warash, B. G. (1989, Winter). Adventures with the globe: Early childhood geography. *Day Care & Early Education, 17*(2) 10–13.

Hawkins, M. (1979–1980, Winter). Teaching map skills in the elementary school. *Indiana Social Studies Quarterly, 32*(3), 33–37.

Hewes, D.W. (1982). Preschool geography: Developing a sense of self in time and space. *Journal of Geography, 81,* 94–97.

Hill, W. (1964). *Curriculum guide for geographic education.* Normal, IL: National Council for Geographic Education.

Joint Committee on Geographic Education. (1984). *Guidelines for geographic education: Elementary and secondary schools.* Washington, D.C.: Association of American Geographers and National Council for Geographic Education.

Kennamer, L. (1963). Developing a sense of place and space. In H. M. Carpenter (Ed.), Skill development in social studies (pp. 148–170). Washington, DC: National Council for the Social Studies.

Kocher, M. B. (1972). *The Montessori manual of cultural subjects.* Minneapolis, MN: Dennison.

Liben, L. S., & Downs, R. M. (1989). Educating with maps: Part I, The place of maps. *Teaching Thinking and Problem Solving, 11*(1), 6–9.

————. (1989). Educating with maps: Part II, The place of children. *Teaching Thinking and Problem Solving, 11*(2), 1–4.

————. (1989). Understanding maps as symbols: The development of map concepts in children. In H.W. Reese (Ed.), *Advances in child development and behavior* (Vol. 22, pp. 145–201). New York: Academic Press.

Melahn, D. (1989, July-August). Putting it in perspective: Geographic activities for primary children. *Journal of Geography, 88*(4), 137–139.

Meyer, J. (1973). Map skill instruction and the child's developing cognitive abilities. *Journal of Geography, 72*(6), 27–35.

Mitchell, L. S. (1971). *Young geographers.* New York: Bank Street College of Education. (Original edition published 1934)

Muessig, R.H. (1987, May). An analysis of developments in geographic education. *The Elementary School Journal, 87*(5), 519–530.

Muir, S.P., & Cheek, H.N. (1983, October). *A developmental mapping program integrating geography and mathematics.* Paper presented at the meeting of the National Council for Geographic Education, Jamaica. (ERIC Document Reproduction Service No. ED 238 796)

————. (1986, April). Mathematics and the map skill curriculum. *School Science and Mathematics, 86*(4), 284–291.

Pagano, A. L. (Ed.). (1978). *Social studies in early childhood: A n interactionist point of view.* (Bulletin 58). Washington, D.C.: National Council for the Social Studies.

Pattison, W.D. (1964, May). The four traditions of geography. *Journal of Geography, 63*(5), 211–216.

Pritchard, S. F. (1989, July-August). Using picture books to teach geography in the primary grades. *Journal of Geography, 88*(4), 126–136.

Rice, G. H. (1990, October). Teaching students to become discriminating map users. *Social Education, 54*(6), 393–397.

Rice, M. J., & Cobb, R. L. (1979). *What can children learn in geography? A review of research.* Boulder, CO: ERIC Clearinghouse for Social Studies/Social Science Education. (ERIC Document Reproduction Service No. ED 166 088)

Richards, L. (1983, October). *Piagetian theory as an organizer for geographic skills and experiences.* Paper presented at the meeting of the National Council for Geographic Education, Jamaica. (ERIC Document Reproduction Service No. ED 241 386)

Scarfe, N. (1965). *Geography in school.* Normal, IL: National Council for Geographic Education.

Seldin, T., & Raymond [Seldin], D. (1981). *Geography and history for the young child: The Montessori approach.* Provo, UT: Brigham Young University Press.

Stoltman, J. (1979–1980, Winter). Geographic skills in the early elementary years. *Indiana Social Studies Quarterly, 32*(3), 27–32.

Stoltman, J. P. (1986). Geographical education and society: Changing perspectives on school geography in the United States. In A. Hernando (Ed.), *Geographical education and society* (pp. 1–11). International Geographical Union Commission on Geographical Education. (ERIC Document Reproduction Service No. ED 284 815).

———. (1991). Research on geography teaching. In J. P. Shaver (Ed.). *Handbook of research on social studies teaching and learning: A project of the National Council for the Social Studies.* (pp. 437–447). New York: Macmillan Publishing Company.

Sunal, C. S. (1987, July-August). Mapping for the young child. *Social Studies, 78*(4), 178–182.

———, & Sunal, D. (1978). Mapping the child's world. *Social Education, 42*(5), 381–383.

Thralls, Z.A. (1958). *The teaching of geography.* New York: Appleton-Century-Crofts.

————, & Reeder, E.H. (1932). *Geography in the elementary school.* New York: Rand McNally and Company.

Van Cleaf, D. W. (1985). The environment as a data source: Map activities for young children. *Social Education, 49*(2), 145–146.

Whipple, G.M. (Ed.). (1933). *The teaching of geography.* (32nd yearbook of the National Society for the Study of Education). Bloomington, IL: Public School Publishing Company.

BIBLIOGRAPHY OF
GEOGRAPHY RESEARCH AND RESOURCES

Books, Book Chapters, Pamphlets

Current

101. Blyth, J. (1984). *Place and time with children five to nine.* London, England: Croom Helm.

    See Chapter 3, Item 303.

102. Debelak, M., Herr, J., & Jacobson, M. (1981). *Creating innovative classroom materials for teaching young children.* New York: Harcourt Brace Jovanovich.

    The authors have created a spiral-bound how-to-do-it book containing numerous ideas for hands-on activities. The chapter on social studies includes step-by-step directions for activities which assist children in the development of spatial and temporal relations concepts, for example, the "landscape cloth," and "what can you do in the dark?"

103. Geographic Education National Implementation Project (GENIP). (1987). *K-6 geography: Themes, key ideas, and learning opportunities.* Macomb, IL: National Council for Geographic Education.

    Designed to promote geographic education and combat geographic illiteracy, this first publication of the Geographic Education National Implementation Project is an aid to the implementation of the *Guidelines* of the Joint Committee on Geographic Education (#104) in grades kindergarten through six. It provides selected examples of learning opportunities related to the key ideas listed in the program overview. Each set of key ideas is in turn related to the central foci for grades K-6, and to the themes in the *Guidelines*. This blueprint for the 1990s reiterates the spiral ideas of Bruner in stating that concepts and skills introduced at an early level become refined through use at successive levels of the curriculum.

Additionally, the authors state that all the themes and key ideas can be introduced in any order at any grade level.

104. Joint Committee on Geographic Education. (1984). *Guidelines for geographic education: Elementary and secondary schools.* Washington, D.C.: Association of American Geographers and National Council for Geographic Education.

This important pamphlet is an authoritative statement regarding the current content, and process, of geographic education. It sets forth and defines five fundamental themes in geography. The role of geographic education and a sequence for presenting geographic concepts in the elementary school is described. A brief section on secondary school geography is included.

105. Lillard, P.P. (1980). *Children learning: A teacher's classroom diary.* New York: Schocken Books.

This diary of a year in the classroom life of Montessori practitioner Paula Polk Lillard gives us deep insights into the Montessori method at work. It demonstrates one teacher's faith in children and in the sequential approach to geography learning based on the needs of the child. An engaging account of the practical application of Montessori cultural subjects and philosophy in an independent day school.

106. Mehlinger, H. D. (Ed.). (1981). *The social studies.* (80th Yearbook). Chicago, IL: National Society for the Study of Education.

107. Pagano, A. L. (Ed.). (1978). *Social studies in early childhood: An interactionist point of view.* (Bulletin 58). Washington, D.C.: National Council for the Social Studies.

Action photographs illustrate this practical social studies handbook, which details the integration of action-oriented pedagogy with developmental theory, problem solving, and citizenship education. The importance of the child, parent, teacher triad is stressed, along with children's use of media. Pagano's concluding chapter summarizes the interactionist

orientation to social studies, including a detailed example of a
practical geography project.

108. Price, G. C. (1982). Cognitive learning in early childhood
education: Mathematics, Science, and Social studies. In B.
Spodek (ed.), *Handbook of research in early childhood
education* (pp. 264–294). New York: The Free Press.

109. Redleaf, R. (1983). *Open the door let's explore: Neighborhood
field trips for young children.* St. Paul, MN: Toys 'n Things
Press.

In this clearly organized, soft-cover curriculum handbook,
local field trips are used as the jumping-off point for classroom
activities in the creative arts, vocabulary development and
language arts, science, and math. Many helpful suggestions
for the teacher are provided. Related discussion topics,
observations, questioning techniques, language arts materials,
and books are linked to each adventure.

110. Schreiber, J.E. (1984). *Using children's books in social studies.*
Washington, D.C : National Council for the Social Studies.

This is a practical guide to the use of children's literature
in the social studies classroom. The introductory essays use
relevant examples to present the author's rationale for the
placement of books in particular concept and skill categories
in the annotated bibliography which follows.

111. Seefeldt, C. (1987). *The early childhood curriculum: A review
of current research.* New York: Teachers College Press.

This book includes reports and discussions of research in
each of the curriculum areas by early childhood education
professionals. In Chapter Ten, "Social Studies in Early
Childhood Education," Blythe Hinitz surveys the social studies
research of the seventies and eighties related to young
children. The chapter provides an in-depth look at historical
perspectives, economic concepts, geography and spatial
relations, and sociology from the viewpoint of recent
literature.

112. Seefeldt, C. (1989). *Social studies for the preschool- primary child.* (3rd ed.). Columbus, OH: Charles E. Merrill.

Seefeldt's comprehensive treatment of social studies for the nursery school, kindergarten and primary-grade student is a major book in print in the field. It is one of two texts which deal exclusively with the appropriate, meaningful presentation of the social sciences to young children. The current edition contains chapters dealing with the nature of and approaches to social studies education, planning and resources, concept formation, history, geography, economics, international education, current topics, attitudes, values, and skills.

Chapter Six presents key geographical concepts dealing with the earth, direction, location, region, spatial arrangements, and maps. Associated projects, resources, materials for children, and references are included.

113. Seldin, T. & Raymond [Seldin], D. (1981). *Geography and history for the young child: The Montessori approach.* Provo, UT: Brigham Young University Press.

This book provides a clear, detailed exposition of Montessori activities related to geography and history. Pertinent photographs amplify the textual material. Succinct reviews of the Montessori approach to education and to the child, the set-up of the Montessori classroom, and lesson planning and presentation in the Montessori school, are included. An extensive bibliography on the Montessori method, geography, and history is provided by the authors.

114. Stanley, W. B. (Ed.). (1985). *Review of research in social studies education: 1976–1983.* (Bulletin 75). Washington, D.C.: National Council for the Social Studies.

The intent of this timely update of a previous bulletin, published jointly by the ERIC Clearinghouse for Social Studies/Social Science Education, the National Council for the Social Studies, and the Social Science Education Consortium, is to explore some important issues related to research in social education. Jantz and Klawitter, in their chapter, "Early

Learning "home geography." Photo by Frances Benjamin Johnston, 1900. Library of Congress.

Childhood/Elementary Social Studies: A Review of Recent Research," discuss the portrayal of the field of social studies for young children in recent publications. Among the topics presented in the chapter are: the social perspective, children's spatial and temporal understandings, concept formation, information processing, and the Piagetian perspective.

115. Sunal, C. S. (Ed.). (1990). *Early childhood social studies*. Columbus, OH: Charles E. Merrill.

Sunal presents a different perspective in this second of the two available volumes which deal with appropriate, meaningful social studies curriculum and methodology for the young child. This teacher education text contains chapters about what the social studies are, the goals of the social studies program, developmental and learning theory, planning for and evaluating children and teaching, the use of resources, multicultural education, values education, history, geography, economics, the elderly and the ill, and death. Three chapters are devoted to different developmental approaches to learning and teaching: the social exploration, experimental, and concept attainment models.

Chapter Twelve defines geography from a developmental viewpoint. It presents specific space concepts and areas of topological study, discussions of block play, maps, globes and map symbols. The chapter concludes with a brief overview of geographic research. References are included.

Classic

116. Bacon, P. (Ed.). (1970). *Focus on geography: Key concepts and teaching strategies*. (40th yearbook). Washington, DC: National Council for the Social Studies.

This sourcebook includes a vast amount of information on theories and trends in geography education and child development, teaching models and methods, and preparation of geography teachers, at the close of the sixties.

117. Ball, J. (1969, April). *A bibliography of geographic education*. Athens, Georgia: Geography Curriculum Project, University of Georgia.

A comprehensive bibliography of articles, books, pamphlets and dissertations in geographic education appearing between 1950 and 1968, produced by a professor of geography education and members of his graduate seminar.

118. Carpenter, H. M. (Ed.). (1963). *Skill development in social studies*. (33rd yearbook). Washington, DC: National Council for the Social Studies.

In Chapter IX, "Developing a Sense of Place and Space," Lorrin Kennamer addresses the geographic contribution to the social studies. The author presents maps, globes, and vocabulary as tools which assist in developing spatial relationship skills. The chapter expands on the list of six basic map and globe skills first promulgated by Clyde F. Kohn in the Twenty-Fourth Yearbook of the National Council for the Social Studies. A listing of activities for the primary, intermediate, junior, and senior high school student is provided. There are suggested activites for the primary (K-3) level in each of the six categories. The chapter concludes with a brief annotated bibliography.

119. Gerhardt, L. (1973). *Moving and knowing: The child orients himself in space*. Englewood Cliffs, NJ: Prentice Hall.

In this classic out-of-print expansion of her doctoral study, Gerhardt relates Piagetian theory, movement studies, and geographical concepts. Included are activities using tile floors, Carolyn Pratt blocks, and box sculptures. Examples from children's guided oral discussion, drawings and floorplans are included. The author's vocabulary and pictorial charts, photographs and reproductions of children's drawings enhance this excellent example of the melding of theory with practice.

120. Hanna, P., Sabaroff, R., Davies, G., & Farrar, C. (1966). *Geography in the teaching of social studies: Concepts and skills*. Boston: Houghton Mifflin.

The sound growth of geographic education as part of a coordinated, multidisciplinary social studies program in the elementary school is the objective of this text. The emphasis espoused for the primary grades is the expanding environments approach, utilizing such firsthand experiences as thoughtful observation, dramatic play, and trips, and the ability to map in some form what has been observed.

121. Hart, R. (1979). *Children's experience of place*. (New York): Irvington Publishers.

122. Henry, N. B. (Ed.). (1957). *Social studies in the elementary school*. (56th Yearbook) Chicago, IL: National Society for the Study of Education.

123. Hill, W. (1964). *Curriculum guide for geographic education*. Normal, IL: National Council for Geographic Education.

124. James, P. E. (Ed.). (1959). *New viewpoints in geography*. (29th yearbook). Washington, DC: National Council for the Social Studies.

Written at the close of the fifties, this volume presents the state of the geographic education program in the United States and the Soviet Union at that time. It details developments in cartography, several approaches to geography, elementary level methods and materials, and teacher preparation programs.

125. Kocher, M. B. (1972). *The Montessori manual of cultural subjects*. Minneapolis, MN: Dennison.

Kocher's book describes several practical life and sensorial activities in the area of geography. Accompanying photographs amplify the descriptions of the materials and procedures given in the text.

126. Kohn, C.F. (Ed.). (1948). *Geographic approaches to social education*. (19th yearbook). Washington, DC: National Council for the Social Studies (NCSS).

This early NCSS publication discusses the philosophy, goals, objectives, and materials used in geography education in the forties. A primary readiness program, and the instructional program used in the elementary, secondary, and teacher education curricula constitute the second section of the book.

127. Kurfman, D. G. (Ed.). (1977). *Developing decision-making skills*. (47th yearbook). Washington, DC: National Council for the Social Studies (NCSS). (ERIC Document Reproduction Service No. ED 049 098)

Chapter three of the final NCSS Yearbook, "Acquiring Information by Asking Questions, Using Maps and Graphs, and Making Direct Observations," by Charlotte Anderson and Barbara Winston, presents considerations related to helping students obtain pertinent information skillfully. Among the geography-related skills and objectives included are: extracting information from prepared sources such as maps, globes, diagrams, charts and graphs; using direct observation experiences; and developing affective outcomes such as self-awareness, respect for others, and world-mindedness.

128. Kurfman, D. G. (Ed.). (1970). *Evaluation in geographic education*. (1971 yearbook of the National Council for Geographic Education). Belmont, CA: Fearon Publishers.

This reference work contains a comprehensive treatment of the evaluation of geographic education at various levels, and of various types. Introductory chapters present the educational purposes of geography, and general developments in the field of evaluation to that date.

129. Manson, G. & Ridd, M. (Eds.). (1977). *New perspectives on geographic education: Putting theory into practice*. Dubuque, IA: Kendall-Hunt.

This volume, produced by the National Council for Geographic Education, synthesizes the work on scope and methodology in geographic education done during the sixties and seventies. The elementary geography education curriculum is examined, and its place in the social studies and science curricula are discussed. Sample lessons designed for immediate classroom use are included in the chapters dealing with the inquiry, expository, values strategy, field, and archival methods. The final chapter contains an excellent overview of selected historical aspects and a noteworthy bibliographic essay on geography in the elementary school. It is a reprint of Manson, G. & Vuicich, G. (1976). *Toward geographic literacy: Objectives for geographic education in the elementary school.* Boulder, CO: Social Science Education Consortium.

130. Mitchell, L. S. (1971). *Young geographers.* New York: Bank Street College of Education. (Original edition published 1934).

A tiny classic filled with gems, this book forms the foundation for much of the primary geography curriculum. The basic tenets set down in 1934 hold true to this day. Mitchell's ideas may have been modified, reworded or amplified, but they have never been discarded, because they are at the heart of the young child's geographic education. The first section of the book expresses the belief that every environment is a geographic environment, that children need to explore their immediate environment through play, and their community through field trips. The view that geography should not be regarded as a separate subject, but rather as a point of view which can color many subjects, was one of the reasons the book was reprinted in 1971, as an example of developmental early childhood philosophy. The second section of the book contains practical suggestions on child and teacher map making and a suggested sequence for map usage by children. Historical photographs, and line drawings, enhance the pages.

131. Robison, H. F. & Spodek, B. (1965). *New directions in the kindergarten.* New York: Teachers College Press.

The concepts and content of the kindergarten program of the sixties are described in this professional publication, based on the doctoral dissertations of the authors. The geography section details a variety of map-related kindergarten experiences.

132. Scarfe, N. (1965). *Geography in school*. Normal, IL: National Council for Geographic Education.

This collection of previously published journal articles was compiled by the National Council for Geographic Education to honor the author, an important geographic educator.

133. Thralls, Z.A. (1958). *The teaching of geography*. New York: Appleton-Century-Crofts.

This classic geography education text of the fifties presents the philosophy and methods used in training an entire generation of elementary school teachers. Its contents integrate mathematics, reading, and current events with geography. Included is a geographic readiness program for grades one to three.

134. Thralls, Z.A. & Reeder, E.H. (1932). *Geography in the elementary school*. New York: Rand McNally and Company.

An early professional methods publication by two important elementary geography educators, this book emphasizes the teaching of units which integrate all the subjects, in the primary grades. The major portion of the book consists of a series of units which encompass the geography-related social studies topics in the elementary curriculum of that period. The final section discusses essential tools and materials for geography instruction, including graphs, specimens, pictures, and "the school journey."

135. Walford, R. (1969). *Games in geography*. London: Longman Group, Ltd.

A collection of games designed for elementary and secondary school use by a Lecturer at Maria Grey College of Education in England, this small volume also discusses geography teaching and gaming theory.

136. Wann, K. D., Dorn, M. S., & Liddle, E. A. (1962). *Fostering intellectual development in young children*. New York: Teachers College Press.

This study of the ways in which children understand their world contains a chapter dealing with the faraway in space and time. Examples of dialogues taken from actual child care settings are helpful in demonstrating three-, four-, and five-year-olds' development of geographic and temporal understandings through play.

137. Whipple, G.M. (Ed.). (1933). *The teaching of geography*. (32nd yearbook of the National Society for the Study of Education). Bloomington, IL: Public School Publishing Company.

This publication contains a vast amount of information on geography and education, geography in the curriculum of the twenties and thirties, and the curriculum in geography of the time. Chapters on the training of geography teachers, and books and materials for classroom use, are provided. The final section is an in-depth review of eighty-two research reports of geography study at all educational levels.

138. Willcockson, M. (Ed.). (1956, January). *Social education of young children: Kindergarten-primary grades*. (Curriculum Series No. 4) (2nd. rev. ed). Washington, D.C.: National Council for the Social Studies.

The fourth edition of this classic publication is divided according to subject area and program. In the chapter on geographical understandings, Sorenson proposes a systematic, flexible program of geography readiness encompassing graded classroom learning experiences and excursions into the community.

139. Willcockson, M. (Ed.). (1952). *Social education of young children: Kindergarten-primary grades*. (Curriculum Series No. 4) (rev. ed). Washington, D.C.: National Council for the Social Studies.

This update of a 1940s publication addresses social education according to experiences deemed appropriate for grade levels kindergarten to three. It includes a discussion of the expanding environments approach as it relates to grade placement of content in the "lower school" by Paul Hanna, a major proponent of that approach.

140. Yardley, A. (1973). Discovering the physical world. New York: Citation Press.

Yardley's sensitive treatment of geography and history from the child's perspective is a plus in this compact book, from the out-of-print Young Children Learning series.

Related ERIC Documents

141. Almy, M. (1967). The psychologist looks at spatial concept formation: Children's concepts of space and time. In National Council for Geographic Education, *Research needs in geographic education: Suggestions and possibilities* (pp. 23–40). Normal, Illinois: Illinois State University. (ERIC Document Reproduction Service No. ED 059 139)

142. deLeeuw, G. [1967]. Contributions of the discipline of geography to the social studies. (ERIC Document Reproduction Service No. ED 066 380)

143. Donaldson, O.F. (1975). *Children are geographers: Explorations in space*. (Instructional activities series IA/E12). Oak Park, IL: National Council for Geographic Education. (ERIC Document Reproduction Service No. ED 124 456)

144. Gifford, E.O. [1972]. Cartographic symbolism and very young children. (ERIC Document Reproduction Service No. ED 062 238)

145. Holtgrieve, D. & Mathiason, C. (1975). *Field trips in geographic education: An annotated bibliography*. Chicago, IL: National Council for Geographic Education. (ERIC Document Reproduction Service No. ED 138 527)

146. Larkin, R.P. & Grogger, P.K. (1975). *Map and compass skills for the elementary school.* (Instructional activities series). Oak Park, IL: National Council for Geographic Education. (ERIC Document Reproduction Service No. ED 138 529)

147. Liben, L.S. & Downs, R.M. (1986, May 31). Perspective-taking in Piagetian and Pennsylvanian landscapes. In R.M. Downs (Chair), *Maps as symbolic representations: Developmental perspectives.* Symposium conducted at the Sixteenth Annual Symposium of the Jean Piaget Society, Philadelphia, PA. (ERIC Document Reproduction Service No. ED 275 392)

148. Manson, G. (1980, April). *An analysis of the status of geography in American schools.* Paper presented at the meeting of the Association of American Geographers (ERIC Document Reproduction Service No. ED 188 972)

149. Muir, S.P. & Cheek, H.N. (1983, October). *A developmental mapping program integrating geography and mathematics.* Paper presented at the meeting of the National Council for Geographic Education, Jamaica. (ERIC Document Reproduction Service No. ED 238 796)

150. Pryer, R. (1977, January). *An evaluation of the Nystrom map and globe study skills program.* Spokane, WA: Spokane School District 81. (ERIC Document Reproduction Service No. ED 155 119)

151. Rice, M. J. & Cobb, R. L. (1979). *What can children learn in geography? A review of research.* Boulder, CO: ERIC Clearinghouse for Social Studies/Social Science Education. (ERIC Document Reproduction Service No. ED 166 1088)

152. Richards, L. (1983, October). *Piagetian theory as an organizer for geographic skills and experiences.* Paper presented at the meeting of the National Council for Geographic Education, Jamaica. (ERIC Document Reproduction Service No. ED 241 386)

153. Stoltman, J. P. (1986). Geographical education and society: Changing perspectives on school geography in the United States. In A. Hernando (Ed.), *Geographical education and society* (pp. 1–11). International Geographical Union Commission on Geographical Education. (ERIC Document Reproduction Serivce No. ED 284 815).

154. Sunal, C. S. & Warash, B.G. (1984, November). *Mapping with young children.* Paper presented at the annual meeting of the National Council for Social Studies, Washington, DC. (ERIC Document Reproduction Service No. ED 248 163)

Conference Proceedings

155. Liben, L.S., Downs, R. & Daggs, D. G. (1988, June 4). *Geographic education: The value of a Piagetian perspective.* Workshop conducted at the Eighteenth Annual Symposium of the Jean Piaget Society, Philadelphia, Pennsylvania.

156. Perry, M.D. & Wolf, D.P. (1986, May 31). Mapping symbolic development. In R.M. Downs (Chair), *Maps as symbolic representations: Developmental perspectives.* Symposium conducted at the Sixteenth Annual Symposium of the Jean Piaget Society, Philadelphia, Pennsylvania.

157. Renninger, K.A. (1985, June). *Object-child relations: A co-constructive perspective of learning processes.* Paper presented at the meeting of the Jean Piaget Society, Philadelphia, PA.

Chapter 2

ECONOMICS

Economic concepts are basic to children's lives. Children in the early years of life have wants and needs. They live in the United States democratic market economy. The task of early childhood teachers, in conjunction with parents, is to help each child move from the basic definition of economics, "how I am supported financially" (Ellis in Pagano, 1978) to a broader and deeper knowledge and understanding of the points detailed below.

1. Since wants are greater than the resources available to satisfy them, individuals must make choices.
2. Some form of economic system determines what goods and services will be produced, how they will be produced, how production will be maintained and increased, and how goods and services will be shared.
3. Specialization tends to increase efficiency and production.
4. Production of goods and services is limited by available resources.
5. All economics have a dynamic system of flows.
6. Private economic decision making is modified through collective (group) or public (government) action.
7. Social inventions include: money, financial institutions (banks, stocks, bonds, commodity markets), business organizations, labor unions and insurance companies.
8. Emergencies can cause some items to be scarce even if all resources are employed. (Warmke, 1980)

Practical classroom examples of all of these concept statements may be found in the literature (Center for Economic Education [Rhode Island], 1988; Naumann, 1976;

Store at the Douglas-Simmons Elementary School, where children learn how to shop under price control regulation. Photo by Roger

Olsen & Perry, 1972; Redleaf, 1983; Yeargen & Hatcher, 1985).

Research has shown that children can understand and use some basic economic concepts as early as preschool, kindergarten, and grade one (Kourilsky, 1981, 1977; Schug, 1987, May). Children enter kindergarten possessing an experience-based economic literacy which they use during their first school years (Hansen, 1985; Senesh, 1963; Weaver, 1965). The literature provides additional evidence to support the contentions that children of different academic ability and socioeconomic levels are capable of learning economic concepts through a variety of instructional methodologies (Kourilsky, 1987, 1983; Kourilsky & Ballard-Campbell, 1984; Kourilsky & Hirschleifer, 1976). However, we must be careful in the selection of the concepts presented at each grade level (Schug, 1987, May). The concepts taught in the early years should be developmentally appropriate (Armento, 1988; Bredekamp, 1986). For example, some young children have demonstrated an understanding of ideas such as scarcity and the purpose of advertising, but no understanding of more advanced types of economic reasoning, such as the concepts of profit and loss (Mugge, 1968; Schug & Birkey, 1985). Studies reported in the professional literature can help us to understand the sequential stages in children's development of economic reasoning about such concepts as: scarcity, decision-making, price, choice, production, specialization, distribution, consumption and savings, demand and supply, trade-offs (opportunity cost), cost-benefit analysis, money, barter, banking and exchange, business organization, business venture, and consumer education.

Fox (1978) found that the centered, static, irreversible thought of the preoperational child has a profound effect on the ability of four to six year olds to make sense of direct experience and formal instruction in economics. They are unable to understand either the reciprocal relationship between a buyer and a seller in a store, or the pricing of items, and view store transactions as merely exchanges of money. When asked about the concept of ownership, young children use circular reasoning in their responses. They make statements such as: "I look around and see that it's mine," or "Because they're mine." Fox reports that there are age-related qualitative changes in children's economic notions, which meet Piaget's criteria for cognitive-developmental stages. The children's responses are qualitatively different at each stage, the stages are sequential, and each stage forms a structured whole.

Schug (1985; 1987, May; 1981) has published several reviews of the literature on children's development of economic thinking. They have formed a foundation for contemporary research. These recent studies have been based on the premises that: children's understanding of basic economic concepts follows a developmental sequence consistent with the cognitive development theory of Piaget, that certain economic concepts can be learned by young children, and that concrete experiences foster the development of economic concepts. For example, Schug and Birkey (1985) designed a study to learn how four to nine year olds understand basic economic concepts. The choice of "unreflective" and "emerging" reasoning categories was influenced by the work of Piaget. "Unreflective" reasoning was characterized by highly literal or tautological responses to questioning, often based on the physical properties of the item. "Emerging" reasoning utilized higher order cognitive skills, was less literal, involved understanding another viewpoint, and was more flexible. It was found that the participants' reasoning was statistically different by grade level (preschool, grade one, grade three). The children's level of economic understanding varied somewhat depending on their experiences. This implies that their reasoning can be enhanced by providing them with further personal economic experiences (Schug & Birkey, 1985).

According to Armento (1988), young children can best demonstrate their comprehension of conceptual knowledge by identifying or naming examples of the concept or by explaining the phenomena in their own words. Giving the definition for a concept is a more difficult cognitive task, which should not be expected of younger learners. Children may be asked to act out or draw the main ideas of economic experiences. They may be asked to identify examples of particular ideas or to group and label experiences.

Jahoda (1979, in Schug, 1986) described three levels through which children move in developing the concept of profit. Until the age of eight years, the children in the study did not demonstrate a grasp of any system. They thought that store purchases were simple rituals. Older children developed the idea of two unconnected systems, in which they understood that the store has to pay for the goods it sells but did not understand that the money used came from the customers, nor that the selling and buying prices differ. By the age of ten they began to develop the idea of two integrated systems, with a relationship between the buying and selling prices.

Economic education is linked to values education. According to Schug (1987, 1980), economic education in the elementary grades teaches an implicit set of values. Economics becomes part of the socialization process which helps children learn how to participate successfully in community life. In a democratic society, children learn the importance of individual freedom to make economic decisions and the idea that individuals are responsible for their own decisions.

The work of Armento, Kourilsky and Schug, among others, has provided us with both the theoretical bases and the specific models for fostering the growth of economic concept learning in early childhood classrooms.

Koeller reported in her 1979 review of the research literature in "K-3 economics education" that the status of economic education in the primary grades had not been documented. In the ensuing decade, several reports and journal articles which appeared have documented the status of primary school economics (see: Bragaw & Hartoonian, 1983; Hansen, 1985; Walstad & Watts in Schug, 1985).

The most comprehensive recent review of the research on economic education in the elementary school appears in the Joint Council on Economic Education publication, *Learning Economics through Children's Stories*, Fifth edition. The authors, agreeing with Senesh (1963), state that with the exception of a handful of studies, all research on economic education in primary grades had been done in the period 1960 to 1985 (Hendricks, Nappi, Dawson, & Mattila, 1986). Senesh points out that the report of the 1960 National Task Force of the American Economic Association alerted the public schools to the existence of an organized body of economic knowledge and urged schools to incorporate this knowledge into the curriculum. Senesh's own project materials, utilizing "organic," experiential curriculum approaches, were published as the *Our Working World* series. This pioneering elementary social studies series of the time was based on the discipline of economics. It called for the teaching of basic social science ideas at every grade level with increasing depth and complexity each year, a "spiral" approach to curriculum. (Bruner 1966, 1977; Robison, 1982; Sanders, 1970; Schwartz & Robison, 1982) It was widely used in the schools during the 1960s and 1970s. Schug and Walstad (1991) cite Larkins and Shaver's (1969) study of the *Our Working World* materials as confirmation of Senesh's optimism that economics is an intellectually appropriate subject for elementary students. Another elementary level economic program, entitled the *Elementary School Economics Project* was developed at the University of Chicago. Students using both of these didactic/materials-based approaches were shown to make significant gains in their economic understanding (Kourilsky, 1987). The doctoral work of Helen Robison, described in her dissertation, *Learning Economic Concepts in the Kindergarten* (1963), was published as a chapter in *New Directions in the Kindergarten* (Robison & Spodek, 1965).

The perceptible increase in economic content at the elementary school level was linked by Bragaw and Hartoonian (1983) to the use of the "Master Curriculum Guides" of the Joint Council on Economic Education [JCEE] (1977, 1988) (Smith, L., 1977), and several other curriculum innovations detailed below. Bragaw and Hartoonian suggest that attention to economic education activities varies with the health of the U.S. economy. Therefore, in the last decade, more emphasis has been placed upon economics because of inflation, unemployment, and recession. Walstad and Watts, reporting on the current status of economics in the K-12 curriculum, noted that parents only asked the schools to teach their children how to handle family finances and how to plan career choices in a competitive economy (in Schug, 1985). However, educators have gone beyond the narrow, "dismal science" base, and economics is now recognized as an important, "basic" subject that is worth teaching in elementary schools. In fact, economics education has become a "hot topic" in many school districts. In half of the states, they are responding to legislation mandating some form of economic education in the schools (Schug, 1987, May).

Where is early childhood economic education now and where is it going?

POSITIVE ASPECTS

Key concepts and understandings from the discipline have recently been identified for teachers (Armento, 1988; Davison, 1977; Economic Core Competencies [Missouri], nd.; Gilliard, Caldwell, Dalgaard, Highsmith, Reinke, & Watts, 1988; Hansen, Bach, Calderwood and Saunders, 1977; Kourilsky, 1978; McCabe, 1975; Walstad & Watts in Schug, 1985). In prior decades, a sense of mission about the importance of economics education caused concerned teachers to accept the assumption that economics simply should be taught in the regular school program, without having a theoretical rationale (Schug, 1981). Further discussion of teacher receptivity to inclusion of economics has been based on the perceived versatility of early childhood and elementary school teachers in comparison to secondary school teachers. Primary level teachers have been lauded for their ability to teach and integrate a full array of subjects as opposed to teaching one specific subject area (Kourilsky, 1981).

Three major instructional approaches have been used in teaching primary school economics (Kourilsky, 1987). The most common of these is the didactic/materials-based approach exemplified by the Senesh materials described above. The technological/media-based approach includes television programs, films, and computer games. The inquiry-oriented/experience based approach may best be exemplified by the Kinder-economy program for grades kindergarten to two (Kourilsky, 1977, Kourilsky & Kehret-Ward, 1984) and the Mini-society program for grades three to six (Kourilsky & Ballard-Campbell, 1984; Kourilsky & Campbell, 1984; Kourilsky & Hirshleifer, 1976). The purpose of these widely researched programs is to have children experience economic concepts in a concrete and direct way (Schug & Walstad, 1991).

A wealth of effective instructional and supplementary materials have been created, and are available. Many of them have appeared in professional magazines and journals. (See, for example: Naumann, 1976; Olsen & Perry, 1972; Paine & Jurmu Arnold, 1983; Schug, 1987, November/December; Sunal, Warash & Strong, 1988; Yeargen & Hatcher, 1985; Zevin, 1980). *Elementary Economist*, a newsletter published several times a year by the Joint Council on Economic Education, presents classroom-tested ideas for grades kindergarten through seven. Other materials have been published in pamphlet or book format. (See for example: Barr,

1985; Center for Economic Education [Rhode Island], 1988; Hendricks, Nappi, Dawson, & Mattila, 1986; Joint Council on Economic Education, 1986; Schug, 1986; Schug, 1982; Schug, 1985; Schug & Beery, 1984; Seefeldt, 1989). The ERIC microfiche collection is the source of many related units and lesson plans. (See, for example: Davis, 1980; P. Fox, 1982; Knauer & Steeves, 1987). Although the majority of the published and unpublished written materials listed for the early childhood or primary level are for grades one to three, there are a few sources which are applicable to younger children. (See for example: Barr, 1985; Seefeldt, 1989; Skeel, 1988; Sunal, et al., 1988).

There are many media-related sources of ideas and teaching methods which teachers can utilize. In recent years television program segments and series have been developed. Saul Barr, a former director of the Maryland Council on Economic Education, was involved in the production of seventy-five economics lesson segments shown on Romper Room, a network television program aimed at young children. The Joint Council on Economic Education has assisted in the production of the television series Trade-offs, and Adventure Economics Series, which are available in several video tape formats (Meszaros, 1978). Computer programs for the presentation and infusion of economic concepts are available, although the majority of the programs are designed for intermediate rather than primary level students. (See reference list below). The use of noncomputer simulations, and multi-disciplinary projects such as the Kinder-economy, has broadened the scope of economic education (Wilson & Schug, 1979). Numerous films and filmstrips are available. The Joint Council on Economic Education periodically updates its publication, *Audiovisual Materials for Teaching Economics* (Harter, Nelson, & Farrell, 1980). New editions are based on the most recent acquisitions received at the National Center for Audiovisual Materials for Teaching Economics at

Oregon State University (Corvallis), or annotated by professional volunteers in the field.

Some school districts have built comprehensive economic curricula which provide the foundation for cumulative increases in students' knowledge of the subject. The statement that elementary curricula are more flexible than secondary curricula has been used to support the inclusion of economics from kindergarten on. A number of elementary schools include economics within the social science curriculum, while others have not yet added it to the structure (Hansen, 1985; Kourilsky 1981; Schug, 1985, 1980; Symmes, 1981). The Developmental Economic Education Program (DEEP) has aided school districts in including, and increasing the quality of, economic instruction. The Joint Council on Economic Education network, through DEEP, provides support for teacher training, curriculum planning, and educational materials. The school district, with the approval of the superintendent, determines its goals in, and establishes a plan for, economic education. The program is organized and a coordinator is chosen. DEEP is implemented through teacher training and the development and revision of curriculum and teaching materials. The process is introduced in grade one and systematically extended to the higher grades. Following evaluation, the change is institutionalized by transforming the pilot project into an integrated part of the ongoing program of the school system (Hahn & Rushing in Symmes, 1981; Walstad & Watts in Schug, 1985). Recent studies have indicated that "students in DEEP districts have statistically higher mean test scores than students from non-DEEP districts, even after controlling for the influence of other major factors" (Schug & Walstad, 1991). A national network of State Councils and University Centers for Economic Education exists to assist teachers and school districts in their efforts. Among the professional services of the state economic education centers are newsletters, publications, audio-visual materials, consulting services and workshops.

Many opportunities are available for teachers to learn more about the subject of economics and related curriculum issues in courses, conferences, and workshops (Walstad & Watts, Laughlin in Schug, 1985). The presentations at conferences and in-service workshops are sources of current information (Sunal, Warash & Strong, 1987). A number of professional organizations, including the National Council for Social Studies (NCSS), the American Home Economics Association (AHEA), the Home Economics Education Association division of the National Education Association (HEEA-NEA), the National Business Education Association (NBEA), the National Association for the Education of Young Children (NAEYC) and the Association for Childhood Education International (ACEI) include opportunities for educators to learn about economics in their professional publications and conference proceedings (Laughlin in Schug, 1985; Swick in Hatcher, 1987).

Appropriate content materials are often provided by business and industry. However, caution should be used in their selection. Although many of the materials are of high quality and help to stretch limited funds, the materials may not always present a balanced view of a topic. Some materials may convey misleading economic information.

Laughlin provides a series of questions which should be asked prior to the adoption of such materials. For example, what critical thinking and decision-making skills will students learn by using this material? Is the material related to the goals and objectives of the local curriculum? Does the material allow for alternative interpretations? Some examples of providers of preschool and primary level curriculum materials which might be surveyed using these questions are: the American Automobile Association, the Rice Council of America, the National Dairy Council, and the American Dental Association. (Laughlin in Schug, 1985)

NEGATIVE ASPECTS

There appears to be a lack of demand, expressed need for, or willingness to provide economics in the K-12 curriculum of some school districts (Hansen, 1985). There is limited time in the school curriculum. Walstad and Watts (in Schug, 1985) report that elementary teachers spend an average of twenty five minutes a day on social studies. Of that, one fifth (twenty five minutes a week) is spent on economics-related topics.

There has been a lack of a wide range of suitable curriculum materials, particularly for the nursery school and kindergarten levels. In fact, in the Fall of 1988, the Joint Council on Economic Education changed the grade level focus of the *Elementary Economist* from Pre-K and 1–2 to K-1 and 2–3, in order to denote a change in the focus of the publication "from preschool/sixth grade to kindergarten/seventh grade. The instructional suggestions provided in the various articles have also been adjusted accordingly." (*Elementary Economist* Vol. 10 No. 1, Fall, 1988, p.1) Publishers often do not include economic skills and concepts in their materials. Textbooks and curriculum series vary considerably in their treatment of economic content. Often it is difficult to determine exactly which concepts are economic (Hansen, 1985; Nappi & Reha 1978). Some developmentally appropriate materials are available but they are often under-used (Koeller, 1979; Walstad & Watts in Schug, 1985).

There is a need for the use of a wider variety of instructional approaches in the primary classroom. In many instances, lecture, provision of reading matter, and worksheets are the only methods used. As mentioned above, ideas for simulations, class discussions, role plays, debates, bulletin boards, teacher-made games, learning centers, and art activities are available. Any or all of them may be used in a variety of ways to stimulate economic thinking (Kourilsky, 1987; Schug, 1980).

The area of evaluation of economic education in the early years has been neglected. Poor evaluation tools, out of date instruments, and the non-use of available tools has led many professionals to ignore this aspect of the economic education program. Evaluation procedures are available, and new ones are being established, even though they need continued refinement (Hansen, 1985). The Primary Test of Economic Understanding (PTEU), developed by Donald Davison in the early seventies, was one of the few standardized tests for primary level students available (Davison & Kilgore, 1971). The PTEU will be replaced by a new primary grade test, currently under development by the Joint Council on Economic Education, in 1991 (Gilliard, personal communication, August 24,1989). Another standardized test for the elementary level is the Basic Economics Test (BET) (1981, revised 1990). It is designed to measure understanding of the economic concepts outlined in the *Framework for Teaching Economics* (Schug & Walsted, 1991).

Much work still needs to be done in the areas of teacher preparation and training. Over two-fifths of the inservice elementary level teachers have no formal economic education. Inadequately trained teachers can be the biggest stumbling block to the infusion of economics into the early childhood curriculum. Studies have demonstrated that economic education programs show greater student gains where teachers are well versed in economics. Therefore, teacher training programs in economic education for the preschool-primary level must be upgraded (Bragaw & Hartoonian, 1983; Hansen, 1985; Nappi & Reha, 1978; Smith, 1977; Walstad & Watts in Schug, 1985; Schug, 1983; Schug, 1981). The Joint Council on Economic Education recommended in 1985 that all elementary school teacher candidates be required to take one basic course in economics. Current training practices do not fulfill these recommendations (Schug & Walstad, 1991). It has been suggested that in-service education is one way to correct the deficiencies, however, only a small percentage of classroom teachers take advantage of in-service offerings in this field.

As has been discussed above, a variety of approaches to teaching economics are both available and effective. Children can learn economic ideas from formal instruction. However, teachers should take into account children's varying levels of economic reasoning and possible misunderstandings. Teachers should be aware of developmentally appropriate practice, based on the research in the area of children's developmental growth, particularly cognitive developmental theory. For example, research on economics teaching confirms that economics learning is facilitated if concepts are presented first in the verbal symbol system and then in integrated graphics. Ample opportunities should be provided for relevant practice of the behaviors that meet the teacher's instructional goals, so that the students can demonstrate the expected behaviors (Kourilsky, 1987; Schug, 1987).

The conclusion drawn by those who have studied primary economics learning and teaching is that children can learn many basic economics concepts in developmentally appropriate ways during their early years. This will help them to become economically literate citizens of our democratic society. The critical importance of the development of economic understandings to these children has been underscored in recent years by events, such as the recent stock market downturn and the growth of unemployment, which impact upon them directly. It is the task of early childhood educators to guide these children toward a broader and deeper understanding of the economic world around us.

REFERENCES

Armento, B.J. (Ed.). (1988). *Scope and sequence for economic education K-12: A proposed framework*. Atlanta, GA: National Specialized Center for Learning Theory and Economic Education. Georgia State University.

Barr, S.Z. (1985). *Lifegames: Activity-centered learning for early childhood education in economics.* Menlo Park, CA: Addison-Wesley Publishing Company.

Bragaw, D. & Hartoonian, M. (1983, January). Economics education in the U.S.-The state of the art. *Social Education, 47*(1), 36–39.

Bredekamp, S. (1986). *Developmentally appropriate practice.* Washington, DC: National Association for the Education of Young Children. [see p.52]

Brenneke, J.S. (1981). *Integrating consumer and economic education into the school curriculum.* New York: Joint Council on Economic Education.

Bruner, J. (1977). Process of education revisited. In G. Haas (Ed.). *Curriculum planning: A new approach.* Boston: Allyn and Bacon.

―――. (1966). *The process of education.* Cambridge, MA: Harvard University Press.

Center for Economic and Marketing Education. (1981). *Elementary economics.* FL: University of Western Florida.

Center for Economic Education. (1988). *Elementary lesson plans* [K-6 individual booklets]. Providence, RI: Rhode Island College and Rhode Island Council on Economic Education.

Dalgaard, B.R., & Schug, M.C. (1983, May-June). Using presidential politics to explore economic issues in social studies. *Social Studies, 74*(3), 100–106.

Davis, M.G. (1980). *Busy as a bee in an economic community: A year long study for first graders in economics.* Normal, IL: National Depository for Economic Education Awards. (ERIC Document Reproduction Service No. ED 241 363.

Davison, D. G. (1977). *Master curriculum guide in economics for the nation's schools. Part II. Strategies for teaching economics Primary level (Grades 1–3).* New York: Joint Council on Economic Education. (also in: ERIC Document Reproduction Service No. ED 164 382)

―――, & Kilgore, J. H. (1971). A model for evaluating the effectiveness of economic education in primary grades. *The Journal of Economic Education, 3* (1), 17–25.

Economic core competencies K-3: A guide for teaching the Missouri core competencies in economics. (nd.). Columbia, MO: The Missouri Council on Economic Education.

Fox, K. (1978, October). The beginning of economic education. *Social Education, 42*(6), 478–481. Also in: *Education Digest, 44* (1979, March), 14–16.

Fox, P. (1982). *Project economic stew: A study of poultry and rice. A third-grade economics project. A bird's eye view of an economic stew: A study of poultry and rice production in Arkansas.* Fayetteville, AR: Asbell Elementary School. (ERIC Document Reproduction Service No. ED 228 133).

Gilliard, J.V. (1989, August 24). Personal communication.

————, Caldwell, J., Dalgaard, B.R., Highsmith, R.J., Reinke, R., & Watts, M. (1988). *Master curriculum guide in economics: Economics: What and when: Scope and sequence guidelines, K-12.* New York: Joint Council on Economic Education.

Hansen, H. S. (1985, Summer). The economics of early childhood education in Minnesota. *Journal of Economic Education, 16*(3), 219–224.

Hansen, W. L., Bach, G. L., Calderwood, J. D., & Saunders, P. (1977). *Master curriculum guide in economics for the nation's schools. Part I. A framework for teaching economics: Basic concepts.* New York: Joint Council on Economic Education. (ERIC Document Reproduction Service No. ED 148 648)

Harter, C.T., Nelson, D.M. & Farrell, J.P. (1980). *Audiovisual materials for teaching economics.* (3rd. ed.). New York: Joint Council on Economic Education.

Hendricks, R.H., Nappi, A.T., Dawson, G.G. & Mattila, M.M. (1986). *Learning economics through children's stories.* (5th. ed.). New York: Joint Council on Economic Education.

Joint Council on Economic Education.(1986). *Children in the marketplace: Lesson plans in economics for grades 3 and 4.* (2nd. ed.). New York: Author.

————. *Elementary Economist.* newsletter. New York.

Knauer, V. & Steeves, R.F. (1987). *Suggested guidelines for teaching units (Grades K-12) on consumers, the economy, and the U.S. Constitution.* Washington, D.C.: Office of Consumer Affairs and Ohio State Department of Education, Columbus. (ERIC Document Reproduction Service No. ED 287 796).

Koeller, S. (1981, May-June). Economics education applied to early childhood. *Childhood Education, 57*(5), 293–6.

————. (1979). *A review of the research in economics in early childhood/elementary education, K-3.* (ERIC Document Reproduction Service No. ED 171 412).

Kourilsky, M. (1974). *Beyond simulation: The mini-society approach to instruction in economics and other social sciences.* Los Angeles, CA: Educational Resource Associates.

————. (1987, Summer). Children's learning of economics: The imperative and the hurdles. *Theory Into Practice, XXVI*(3), 198–205.

————. (1981, March-April). Economic education: Making the most of the curriculum. *Social Studies, 72*(2), 86–89.

————. (1983). *Mini-society: Experiencing real-world economics in the elementary school classroom.* Menlo Park, CA: Addison-Wesley Publishing Company.

————. (1978). *Part II: Strategies for teaching economics: Intermediate level (Grades 4–6).* New York: Joint Council on Economic Education.

————. (1986, Summer). School reform: The role of the economic educator. *Economic Education, 17*(3), 213–217.

————. (1977). The kinder-economy: A case study of kindergarten pupils' acquisition of economic concepts. *The Elementary School Journal, 77*(3), 182–191.

————. (1976, September). *The kinder-economy: A case study of kindergarten pupils' acquisition of economic concepts.* Paper presented at the meeting of the Allied Social Science Associations, Atlantic City, NJ.

————, & Ballard-Campbell, M. (1984, September-October). Mini-society: An individualized social studies program for children of low, middle and high ability. *Social Studies, 75*(5), 224–228.

————, & Campbell, M. (1984, January). Sex differences in a simulated classroom economy: Children's beliefs about entrepreneurship. *Sex-Roles: A Journal of Research, 10*(1–2), 53–66.

————, & Hirshleifer, J. (1976). Mini-society vs. token economy: An experimental comparison of the effects on learning and autonomy of socially emergent and imposed behavior modification. *Journal of Educational Research, 69,* 376–381.

————, & Keheret-Ward, T. (1984, January). Kindergartners' attitudes toward distributive justice: experiential mediators. *Merrill-Palmer Quarterly, 30*(1), 49–63.

Mackay-Smith, A. (1985, January 4). Economics 101 goes to the first grade and kids eat it up. *The Wall Street Journal,* p.1.

McCabe, M.F. (1975). *Teachers guide to economic concepts.* Vermillion, SD: Center for Economic Education, South Dakota University and South Dakota Council on Economic Education. (ERIC Document Reproduction Service No. ED 113 272).

Meszaros, B. (1978). *A guide to trade-offs.* Bloomington, IN: Agency for Instructional Television.

Mugge, D. (1968, February). Are young children ready to study the social sciences? *Elementary School Journal, 68*(5), 232–240.

Nappi, A.T., & Reha, R.K. (1978, March). What every elementary school teacher should know about economics. *Elementary School Journal, 78*(4), 242–246.

Naumann, N. ((1976). Nineteen entrepreneurs and one bullish teacher. *Learning, 4*(7), 18–24.

Olsen, H.D., & Perry, L.S. (1972, March). Applied economics: Consumers and producers. *Instructor, 81*(7), 42.

Pagano (1978). *Social studies in early childhood: An interactionist point of view.* Washington, DC: National Council for the Social Studies.

Paine, C., & Jurmu Arnold, A. (1983, January). Contemporary issues for young citizens: Teaching about economics. *Learning: The Magazine for Creative Teaching, 11*(6), 82–83, 86, 88.

Redleaf, R. (1983). *Open the door let's explore: Neighborhood field trips for young children.* St. Paul, MN: Toys'n Things Press.

Robison, H. F. (1983). *Exploring teaching in early childhood education.* (2nd ed.). Boston: Allyn & Bacon.

————, & Spodek, B. (1965). *New directions in the kindergarten.* New York: Teachers College Press.

Sanders, N.M. (1970, April). Experiment in economic education, Purdue University. *Social Education, 34*, 423–425.

Schug, M. C. (1987, May). Children's understanding of economics. *Elementary School Journal, 87*(5), 507–518.

————. (1982). *Economic education across the curriculum.* (Fastback 183). Bloomington, IN: Phi Delta Kappa Educational Foundation. (ERIC Document Reproduction Service No. ED 223 503).

————. (1986). *Economics for kids: Ideas for teaching in the elementary grades.* Washington, DC: National Education Association and The Joint Council on Economic Education.

————. (Ed.). (1985). *Economics in the school curriculum, K-12.* Washington, DC: National Education Association and The Joint Council on Economic Education. (ERIC Document Reproduction Service No. ED 267 002).

————. (1983, Spring). Elementary teachers' views on economic issues. *Theory and Research in Social Education, 11*(1), 55–64.

————. (1987, November-December). Getting started teaching the economics of the Constitution. *Social Studies, 78*(6), 249–254.

————. (1983, February). The development of economic thinking in children and adolescents. *Social Education, 47*(2), 141–145.

————. (1981, Fall). What educational research says about the development of economic thinking. *Theory and Research in Social Education, 9*(3), 25–36.

————. (1980, October). What type of economics program is best for your school? *Educational Leadership, 38*(1), 61–62.

————, & Beery, R. (Eds.). (1984). *Community study: Applications and opportunities.* (Bulletin No. 73). Washington, DC: National Council for the Social Studies. (also in: ERIC Document Reproduction Service No. ED 252 452).

————, & Birkey, C. J. (1985, April). *The development of children's economic reasoning.* Paper presented at the meeting of the American Educational Research Association, Chicago, IL.

————. (1985, Spring). The development of children's economic reasoning. *Theory and Research in Social Education, XIII*(1), 31–42.

————, & Walstad, W. B. (1991). Teaching and learning economics. In J. P. Shaver (Ed.). *Handbook of research on social studies teaching and learning: A project of the National Council for the Social Studies.* (pp. 411–419). New York: Macmillan Publishing Company.

Schwartz, S. & Robison, H. F. (1982). *Designing curriculum for early childhood.* Boston: Allyn & Bacon.

Seefeldt, C. (1989). *Social studies for the preschool-primary child.* (3rd. ed.). Columbus, OH: Charles E. Merrill.

Senesh, L. (1963, March). The economic world of the child. *Instructor, 73,* 7–8.

Smith, L. (1977, January). Keynes goes to kindergarten. *Dun's Review, 109,* 42–43.

Skeel, D.J. (1988). *Snall-size economics: Lessons for the primary grades.* Glenview, IL: Scott, Foresman and Company.

Sunal, C.S., Warash, B.G., & Strong, M. (1988, Summer). Buy! Sell! Produce! Economic education activities. *Day Care and Early Education, 15*(4), 12–15.

————. (1987, November 14). *Economic education for young children and their parents.* Paper presented at the annual meeting of the National Association for the Education of Young Children, Chicago, IL.

Swick, K.J. (1987). The school-workplace interface: Extending basic learning through an ecological approach. In B. Hatcher (Ed.). *Learning opportunities beyond school*. (pp.33–38). Washington, DC: Association for Childhood Education International.

Symmes, S.S. (1981). *Economic education: Links to the social studies*. Washington, DC: National Council for the Social Studies.

Warmke, R.F. (1980, October). Economics. In Rogers & Muessig. Social studies: What is basic? A symposium. *Teacher 98*, 46–47.

Weaver, V.P. (1965, Fall). Social concepts for early childhood education. *Educational Leadership 22*(5), 296–99, 343.

Wilson, C. & Schug, M.C. (1979). *A guide to games and simulations for teaching economics*. (3rd. ed.). New York: Joint Council on Economic Education and University of Minnesota Center for Economic Education.

Yeargen, H., & Hatcher, B. (1985, March/April). The cupcake factory: Helping elementary students understand economics. *The Social Studies*, 76(2), 82–84.

Zevin, J. (1980, April). Visual economics: Inquiry through art and artifacts. *Peabody Journal of Education*, 57, 183–190.

Computer Programs

Lublin, B. & Lipscomb, N. *Nursery rhyme economics*. Richmond, VA: Collegiate Schools.

———. *Potholder business*. Richmond, VA: Collegiate Schools.

Money master. Woodcliff Lake, NJ: Micromedia K-12.

Piggy Bank. New York: Joint Council on Economic Education.

Talafuse, M. *Choices*. Muncie, IN: Center for Economic Education. Ball State University.

———. *Trade-offs*. Muncie, IN: Center for Economic Education. Ball State University.

BIBLIOGRAPHY OF
ECONOMICS RESEARCH AND RESOURCES

Current

201. Armento, B.J. (Ed.). (1988). *Scope and sequence for economic education K-12: A proposed framework*. Atlanta, GA: National Specialized Center for Learning Theory and Economic Education. Georgia State University.

    This spiral-bound volume differs from #207 by offering a more detailed picture of the construction of economic concepts. The first section identifies the five major themes which are the thread tying the book together, with their associated goals. The details of developing objectives by considering the difficulty levels of concepts, organizing the concepts and skills in a sequence from easy to difficult, and applying the theory and research on learning and child development, are discussed. A chart presents the early childhood phase as a stage of informal concept construction in which children can indicate their understanding through oral expression, art activity, role play and/or grouping and labeling experiences. The major economic concepts taught in grades K-4 are listed in the next section. These are followed by a listing of developmentally-appropriate instructional objectives for the same grades. The final section lists the objectives for each grade separately. A kindergarten teacher could use this section to plan the gradual introduction of activities related to the four objectives listed, over the course of the year.

202. Barr, S.Z. (1985). *Lifegames: Activity-centered learning for early childhood education in economics*. Menlo Park, CA: Addison-Wesley Publishing Company.

    This useful handbook includes a wide selection of economics activities designed for children in grades kindergarten to three. The lessons help young children relate their own experiences with goods and services, specialization and jobs, resources, and money and banking to the presentation of those concepts in the classroom. Each lesson contains step-by-step prose directions plus a photograph of children engaging in the activity. The author addresses concepts presented in the *Master Curriculum Guide in Economics for the Nation's Schools* in a developmentally appropriate way.

203. Center for Economic Education. (1988). *Elementary lesson plans* [K-6 individual booklets]. Providence, RI: Rhode Island College and Rhode Island Council on Economic Education.

   Emphasizes the goal of economic education in the elementary school, "to help children become effective decision makers and responsible citizens." Each grade level booklet provides twenty-five lesson plans designed to teach economics through the language arts. The lesson plans are tied to recent scope and sequence guidelines by the competency and learner outcome statements. Child and teacher references are included.

204. Davison, D. G. (1977). *Master curriculum guide in economics for the nation's schools. Part II. Strategies for teaching economics Primary level (Grades 1–3)*. New York: Joint Council on Economic Education. (also in: ERIC Document Reproduction Service No. ED 164 382)

   One in a series of volumes dealing with grades one to twelve, this book provides examples of primary level classroom-tested lesson activity plans for six economic concepts. The suggested instructional activities are designed to serve as tools for primary teachers and supervisors to use in their development of a locally applicable curriculum document. Each activity follows the master format, including a concept statement, needed materials, a rationale, related economic concepts, instructional objectives, teacher strategy, pupil activity, and evaluation. Sample evaluation and review items, a glossary, and a listing of supplementary materials are included in the appendices. This series is currently undergoing revision by the committees of the Joint Council on Economic Education. The projected publication date for the revised volumes is 1991.

205. *Economic core competencies K-3: A guide for teaching the Missouri core competencies in economics.* (nd.). Columbia, MO: The Missouri Council on Economic Education.

   A compilation of economic competencies and learner outcomes listed according to grade levels.

206. Gilliard, J.V., Caldwell, J., Dalgaard, B.R., Highsmith, R.J., Reinke, R., & Watts, M. (1988). *Master curriculum guide in economics: Economics: What and when: Scope and sequence guidelines, K-12.* NY: Joint Council on Economic Education.

   A companion volume to #207, this publication is designed to help school systems develop a comprehensive economic education program. The questions: "What are the fundamental concepts and generalizations that an economically literate person should know?" and "At what grade levels should those concepts and generalizations be introduced and developed?" are explored. The development of basic economic concepts is charted in Part I. In Part II content statements are listed in the order in which they should be introduced into the primary curriculum. Part III groups the content statements by grade level (K-1, 2–3, etc). Behavioral objectives useful for assessment purposes and resource materials available from the Joint Council on Economic Education are provided for each content statement in Part III.

207. Hansen, W. L., Bach, G. L., Calderwood, J. D., & Saunders, P. (1977). *Master curriculum guide in economics for the nation's schools. Part I. A framework for teaching economics: Basic concepts.* New York: Joint Council on Economic Education. (ERIC Document Reproduction Service No. ED 148 648)

   Provides the framework for current economic education practices in our schools. The major elements of economic understanding identified and described are: practicing a reasoned rather than emotional approach to thinking about economic issues, mastering the basic concepts and facts, possessing an overview of the workings of the economy, identifying the issues and applying reasoning and knowledge to those issues, and forming judgments and reaching decisions on economic issues. Concepts articulated in the book are clustered as: basic economic concepts, economic institutions, measurement concepts, and concepts for evaluating economic actions and policies. This volume serves as the foundation for the multivolume *Master Curriculum Guide in Economics (MCG)* series.

208. Harter, C.T., Nelson, D.M., & Farrell, J.P. (1980). *Audiovisual materials for teaching economics*. (3rd ed.). NY: Joint Council on Economic Education.

This comprehensive annotated bibliography of films, filmstrips, and videocassettes supplies information on supporting materials such as cassettes, records, books, workbooks, games, and teacher's guides. The criteria for inclusion of specific items were: economic content and use of the tools of economic analysis, objectivity, effectiveness as a teaching tool to stimulate interest, and wide availability in the United States. Entries for the primary grades (k-3) appear at the beginning of each section.

209. Hendricks, R.H., Nappi, A.T., Dawson, G.G., & Mattila, M.M. (1986). *Learning economics through children's stories*. (5th ed.). NY: Joint Council on Economic Education.

In addition to an expanded listing of children's books related to economics, with suggestions for their instructional use, this volume includes an articulate historical review of the research on economic education in the elementary school from 1930 to 1980; an annotated bibliography of selected relevant articles; lists of journals, bulletins, and other bibliographies of children's stories; and a list of related professional organizations. Featured in chapter three are recently published stories available in bookstores or libraries which met the authors' definition of a story, had a reading level suitable for grades K-6, illustrated economic concepts or principles, and had general applicability to a part of the elementary school curriculum. This publication is based on the collection housed at the National Depository of Children's

Stories in Economics, Center for Economic Education, St. Cloud State University, Minnesota.

210. Joint Council on Economic Education. (1986). *Children in the marketplace: Lesson plans in economics for grades 3 and 4.* (2nd. ed.). NY: Author.

A group of eight lesson plans which touch children in Piaget's concrete operational stage. The lessons are designed to bring an economic way of thinking into the third grade curriculum, by providing the opportunity for students to hear about, apply, experience and review a concept. In accordance with learning theory, the students are then encouraged to generalize the application of the concept to concrete situations.

211. Redleaf, R. (1983). *Open the door let's explore: Neighborhood field trips for young children.* St. Paul, MN: Toys 'n Things Press. (Item 108)

Includes trips to such sources of economic content as the bank, the car dealership, the supermarket, the hardware store, the lumber yard, the service station, and the restaurant.

212. Schug, M. C. (1986). *Economics for kids: Ideas for teaching in the elementary grades.* Washington, DC: National Education Association and The Joint Council on Economic Education.

A helpful guide to economics education ideas for the elementary grades, this book is designed to aid teachers in the initiation of instruction. An overview of the way children think about economic ideas is provided. This is followed by a listing of points to consider when choosing a teaching activity. The major portion of the book is devoted to examples of lesson plans and simulations which answer the conceptual questions posed in chapter one. The concluding chapter discusses guest speakers, field trips and interviews as examples of the fun and excitement that can be generated by using the resources of the local community in teaching economics.

213. ———. (Ed.). (1985). *Economics in the school curriculum, K-12.* Washington, DC: National Education Association and The

Joint Council on Economic Education. (ERIC Document Reproduction Service No. ED 267 002)

An edited volume that is organized into three sections detailing the current status of economics, and the teaching of economics, by grade level, and across the curriculum. In part one, chapter three, Schug identifies the specific economic principles which should be understood by an economically literate individual. In part two, chapter four, Schug and Armento examine children's informal and formal economic experiences, detailing several methods of building upon those experiences. Part three discusses economics and the local and world communities. Chapter nine identifies economic education opportunities for teachers.

214. ———. (1982). *Economic education across the curriculum.* (Fastback 183). Bloomington, IN: Phi Delta Kappa Educational Foundation. (ERIC Document Reproduction Service No. ED 223 503)

This fastback from the Phi Delta Kappa series sets forth the author's definition of economic education and a rationale for the study of economics. Sections of the slim volume provide examples of economic education in the elementary curriculum and promising approaches to teaching economics. The author cites criteria for the evaluation and use of sponsored curriculum materials in both prose and checklist formats. An appendix listing selected economic education organizations and providers of teaching materials completes the pamphlet.

215. ———, & Beery, R. (Eds.). (1984). *Community study: Applications and opportunities.* (Bulletin No. 73.). Washington, DC: National Council for the Social Studies. (ERIC Document Reproduction Service No. ED 252 452)

Chapter three of this edited publication reviews several approaches to teaching community economics. The author argues that even the youngest children receive weekly allowances, are bombarded by media advertising, accompany adults on shopping trips, and make economic decisions. Schug provides teachers with ideas for making "the abstract concrete and the dull interesting by focusing on the local community."

216. Seefeldt, C. (1989). *Social studies for the preschool- primary child.* (3rd. ed.). Columbus, OH: Merrill Publishing Company.

See Chapter 1, item 112.

Chapter Seven presents such key economic concepts as scarcity, including wants, needs and decision making; and production, including the consumer, goods, services, and using money. Associated projects, resources and references are included.

217. Sunal, C. S. (1990). *Early childhood social studies.* Columbus, OH: Merrill Publishing Company.

See Chapter 1, item 115.

218. Symmes, S.S. (Ed.). (1981). *Economic education: Links to the social studies.* Washington, DC: National Council for the Social Studies.

An edited compendium of ideas on the relationship between social and economic education by noted professionals in both fields. Included are chapters dealing with economic literacy, decision-making, and ideology. Resources for building and evaluating an effective economic education program are introduced. Reading materials and alternative modes of teacher education are discussed. The bulletin concludes with the presentation of persistent economic education problems and some perspectives regarding their resolution.

219. Wilson, C., & Schug, M.C. (1979). *A guide to games and simulations for teaching economics.* (3rd ed.). NY: Joint Council on Economic Education and University of Minnesota Center for Economic Education.

This pamphlet is an informative treatment of the literature on choosing, using, and evaluating games and simulations in the social sciences in general and economics in particular. Materials annotated in the central portion of the publication were chosen on the basis of: meeting the definition of an educational simulation, a learning game, or a simulation/game; involving the use of economic concepts, goals or behavior; applicability to many educational situations; and public availability. Although the majority of the citations are designed for older students, there are several elementary level items which could serve as models for designing one's own simulation or game. A list of available bibliographies, journals, newsletters and publishers of educational games and simulations is found in the concluding chapter. This publication is based on the collection housed at the Specialized Center for Games and Simulations in Economics, Center for Economic Education, University of Minnesota.

Chapter 3

HISTORY

History, in the view of the young child, consists of "my past," according to Pagano (1978). Burnes (1983) states that a personal knowledge of our past gives us identity as individuals. This can be interpreted in different ways depending upon the developmental stage of the child. For the youngest, the concept may be limited to today, yesterday, and tomorrow. For slightly older children, it may be extended to the study of the child's family, stretching several generations into the past; or to the clothing, utensils, toys, musical instruments, and tools used locally decades ago. In the later primary school years, study may be extended to the past of the "human family" (the human race). It can consist of examining different time periods and civilizations in a variety of ways. Of particular relevance is the study of the history of childhood, which can encompass such diverse subject matter as adult perceptions of childhood, infanticide and child abuse, and the changing role of children in the family and the workplace (Downey, 1986).

History has been defined as the memory of things said and done (Becker in Marty, 1983), and the interpretation of things said and done (Burnes, 1983). Thornton (1987) stated that history deals with continuity and change over time. It may divided into social, environmental, and political history, with the first two having greater relevance for the primary level student than the last (Ross, 1986). According to Slater (1978), history remains the one discipline in the curriculum that is concerned with the behaviour of human beings who have actually lived, or indeed who may still be alive. Ross

A seven-year-old's view of time. From *History in Primary Schools* by Joan Blyth, 1989, Open University Press, p. 19. Reprinted by permission.

tells us that history is a way of investgating, a process of thinking, and a capacity to respond. The past, according to Marty, is not some inert mass of factual content lying there waiting to be absorbed. It is a product that historians, including students acting as historians, have created and continue to recreate, using the raw materials of humankind's collective memory to make the past a part of the living present. The historian does not simply investigate and collect the facts, the "what" of history, but is concerned with human motivations, the "why." Students must engage themselves in the activities of historians at a level of sophistication appropriate to their abilities (Marty, 1983). According to Seefeldt (1989), young children can use the methods of the historian to interpret and understand the past. Ellis (1991), in the most recent edition of his teacher education text, cites numerous examples of student-initiated historical research. Schug and Beery (1987) report the belief of Lavelle and Rosenzweig that history should be viewed as a method of studying about the past in a very concrete manner. They contend that social history—history of work, leisure, and family—can provide a rich context for children to develop their own concepts in history. The study of history is related to understanding of time. However, the relationship between temporal and historical learning is poorly understood (Thornton, 1987). Piaget's discussions of intuitive time (successions and durations given by direct perception), and operational time (which involves the use of logic) have been used as a theoretical basis for developing related temporal and historical understandings (Hinitz, 1987). Elkind (1981), identified clock time, calendar time, and psychological time as areas important in children's development of time concepts. In relation to psychological time, Elkind suggests that whatever is taught to children should be tied to their desire to learn more about themselves and their immediate surroundings. Thornton and Vukelich (1988) state that clock time involves using numerical notations to estimate or accurately judge units of time of a clock, watch or digital device. Calendar time requires one to use time language involving days, weeks, months, seasons, holidays, and years, as well as numerical digits, to judge units of time on standard calendars. It can thus be seen that there are many different aspects of time, including past, present, and future; conventional clock and calendar time; duration of physical processes; historical succession and duration (Downey & Levstik, 1991).

A plastic egg timer, an hourglass, and a spring-wound kitchen timer allow the child to actually see the passage of time by watching the movement of the sand or handle. Making and using a sundial, or a water or candle clock teaches scientific concepts as well as temporal ones (Yardley, 1973). Children between the ages of four and six years can be taught to read a (non-digital) clock or watch correctly, however their internalization of the duration of the intervals, the extension to "real time," takes longer to develop. Montessori-based clock activities such as those described by

Seldin and Raymond (1981) assist in this process. Poster (1973) states that a sense of physical time is a necessary but not sufficient ingredient of a sense of the past. He says that historicality, a sense of existing in the past as well as the present, a feeling of being in history rather than standing apart from it, is lacking.

Historical time, as described by Thornton and Vukelich (1988) requires one to depict a person, place, artifact, or event in the past using some form of time language. The language may be as simple as, for example, "back then," or as complex as "late eighteenth century." However, according to Poster (1973), historical time is reconstructed according to the criteria of present societies and groups, which is the reason historians are driven to a constant rewriting of history, rendering historical time both more alive and more ideological. In a study of 480 elementary level students ages six to thirteen, Poster found that children could understand time as related to historical events (they had a sense of order and sequence), but were confused about time relationships which pertained to them or their environment. He concluded that children do not develop a sense of historical time in the neat predictable way we have thought. He therefore proposed that the school history sequence be "turned on its head," so that the distant past would be studied during the early years. Blyth (1984) asserts that the extension of time involves understanding of sequence (the ordering of events), the age of people and objects, language (such as "old" and "century"), actual historical dates (and how they differ from telephone numbers), and the whole concept of the past and how different it is from the present.

Hands-on activities assist in the development of concepts of calendar time and sequencing. Cooking experiences which require a period of heat or cold for the completion of a physical or chemical change are an ongoing part of the early childhood curriculum. Posting the daily schedule in both words and pictures on the classroom wall helps the children to internalize the sequence. Other possibilities for broadening the child's historical understandings include: making and using static and interactive time lines, producing a family tree, implementing the calendar curriculum developed by Lassar Gotkin (1967), and visiting near and distant "places in the past." Field work and museum visits have been invitingly described by Blyth in her several books (1984, 1988, 1989), as well as by Goss (1986), Hatcher (1987), and Richardson (1986). Finkelstein and Nielsen (1985) utilized hands-on activities to teach some historical concepts associated with a centennial in Iowa. Model-making and the use of artifacts from school collections, or borrowed from family, friends or museums, add to the enjoyment of learning historical concepts. West (1978) describes the incorporation of a central collection of artifacts, related stories, and picture slides into the syllabus for six to ten year old children in one British Local Education Authority (LEA). The classroom discussion of the objects, the use of primary evidence such as original documents, and the inclusion in the slides of a variety of fine art works and photographs, assisted the students in gaining a "'sense of evidence of the past' rather than the study of 'history' as such." In the British schools, teacher- or child-made notebooks record the writing, time lines, photos and other illustrative work made by children.

Children's perceptions of physical time have been assumed to constrain historical thinking. However, according to Downey and Levstik (1991), studies indicate that young children can and do understand historical time in a variety of ways. Children see patterns and sequences in real events, though some of these patterns may be general and imprecise. Young children were able to use broad time categories in describing times past (e.g. "cave times" or "before Mom and Dad were born"). By ages eight and nine, children were able to estimate how long ago events took place, to place events in sequence, and to associate dates with particular people and events. Children have demonstrated an understanding of a range of logical relationships, including causal and temporal relations, much earlier than previously thought. They can discuss a range of logical relationships when those relationships are embedded in a script or schema ·that is familiar to them. Indeed, by the time children are five to seven years old they appear to be able to use spatio-temporal knowledge flexibly and explicitly (Downey & Levstik, 1991).

Thornton and Vukelich (1988) have summarized four views of the time/history interdependency (the way in which children's understanding of time concepts affects their understanding of history). They have called them the developmental cognitive view, the psychosocial/developmental view, the organic curriculum view, and the developmental historical time viewpoint. The first two viewpoints are founded upon the work of Piaget and posit the belief that what children can learn about time and history is subject to developmental constraints. Full understanding is dependent upon the child's reaching the stage of formal operations. Egan (1982) disagreed, stating that, "The general image of conceptual poverty in young children, suggested by the developmental theories, sits uneasily with our common observations of children's vivid mental lives."

A third view is only incidentally concerned with developmental theories. It begins with practical questions of curriculum and instruction in the social studies. Its proponents believe that time is mastered in the contexts of "social problems that have meaning and purpose for" children. This problem-centered approach concludes that, given appropriate tasks about "the past that interests" children, important time and history learning is possible even in the lower elementary grades.

The fourth viewpoint, that of Thornton and Vukelich, synthesizes aspects of the other three views. They agree that children's ability to understand time corresponds closely to their cognitive development. However, they interpret the statement to mean that certain historical time and history concepts are within the limits of children as young as six, and that each concept should be taught systematically and reasonably sequentially. They believe that time understanding should be a major consideration in how historical topics are introduced. Therefore, what we say about the past should be considered from the standpoint of the child's understanding of the time language. For example, the past-present dichotomy can be introduced any time after four years of age and most children by age five or six can be introduced to the cyclical nature of events by starting with those in their immediate life. Blyth (1984) suggests that vocabulary lists of "evidence, story, time periods, and other historical terms" be introduced into children's work at the appropriate times. She states that such words should be used with "precision rather than generality, . . . [so that] by the age of 9 children should be able to 'use a specialised [*sic*] vocabulary for historical artefacts [*sic*] and events.'"

Historical time concepts should be taught in conjunction with history just as clock and calendar time are taught in conjunction with math. Historical time language should be taught in social studies courses as carefully as historical information, although it is unclear what impact the time line has on children's understanding of historical time.

Illustrations of all types and text and trade books can be helpful in whetting children's appetites for historical study. Of particular interest are works of historical fiction that are specifically written for children. In fact, the Bradley Commission (1989) members were concerned that teachers be left free to choose engaging books with memorable content, and to tap the same vein of curiosity and imagination that popular culture recognizes and exploits for commercial gain. Agreeing with Preston and Herman, they stated that teachers of young children should be encouraged to be storytellers and dramatists, not just monitors of basal readers or sociologists of the neighborhood. Thus, another appropriate method of initiating historical work is the oral reading or telling of stories by the teacher, an adult guest, or an older student. Use of this technique leads to open-ended questioning and class discussion. A further extension might be the collection of oral history gathered from older relatives or senior citizens in the community. This may lead to continued intergenerational contacts between the center or school and older persons with whom many of the children might not otherwise come into contact. (See: McDuffie & Whiteman, 1987; Perschbacher, 1984; Seefeldt, 1989; Seefeldt & Warman, 1990; Sunal, 1990.)

Historical concepts and temporal relations, if taught at all, are often linked with geographic concepts, in early childhood curricula and literature. Reed (1989), for example, in a discussion of teaching methods and strategies, opines that, "students should understand the relationship between geography and history as a matrix of time and place, and as a context for events." She goes on to discuss the influence of a place and its distinguishing characteristics on an event, and the use of "place" as a category on data collection charts used for the classification of early civilizations.

Although all may agree that the teaching of history is important to enhance students' comprehension of their social environment, and that history is valuable not only as a record of past events, but also as a means for understanding the present structure of society, there is little information on how this can be done (Hinitz, 1987). There is a dearth of readily available written material dealing with history and the young child in particular, and little research on history teaching in general (Downey & Levstik, 1991). A major portion of the English language teacher education literature in this field consists of books written by British authors. In the United States, the two teacher education texts devoted exclusively to early childhood social studies each includes one chapter devoted to the teaching of history. Occasional articles on the subject have appeared in periodicals in the United States and England. Perhaps one reason for the paucity of available information is the prevalence of the "expanding horizons" approach to social studies, which emphasizes the areas of sociology and economics over that of history. At the present time, social studies curricula in the United States are in a state of flux because of the 1989 report of the Bradley Commission and the 1987 California history-social science framework, which challenge the ninety-year supremacy of the "expanding horizons" approach.

In 1987 the Bradley Commission was established to review the status of history in U.S. school curricula and to make recommendations for its improvement. Composed of respected historians and master classroom teachers from elementary and secondary levels, the Commission developed *Building a History Curriculum: Guidelines for Teaching History in Schools* and sponsored a book of essays, *Historical Literacy: The Case for History in American Education.* (*History Matters*)

The members of the Bradley Commission examined past practice and sought input from scholars in several fields. They found that an elementary school curriculum in history, geography and civics for the primary grades, did exist through the early 1900s. According to Ravitch (1987, 1989), children were introduced to exciting stories of important events and significant individuals, to provide them with a basic historical and cultural vocabulary. The curriculum included "home geography," which taught about the neighborhood and the local community. The 1909 report of The Committee of Eight of the American Historical Association described a specific curriculum for the study of history which influenced many school districts. This document included the expectation that primary school children would receive "definite impressions that may be conveyed to them by means of pictures, descriptions, and illustrative stories . . . " (Ravitch, 1981).

In the early 1900s, developmental psychology based on the recapitulation theories of G. Stanley Hall, Herbartian philosophy, and anthropological theory gained prominence with educators. Charles McMurry, a major Herbartian, made no specific recommendations for formal history instruction in grades one and two in his text *Special Method in History*. For third grade he recommended historical stories related to holidays and national celebrations. The introductory remarks in this text hint that fairy tales and myths were appropriate curricula for the early school years (LeRiche, 1987).

The unification movement, which eliminated separate subject matter classifications, was based on the major developmental and philosophical theories of the time. Proponents of unity of knowledge believed that primary grade teachers should not be specialists, but rather "should have a 'rich store of information and accomplishments drawn from all sides, from nature and art, from history and literature'" (Guillet 1900, in Akenson, 1987). This was the beginning of the unified field of social studies, which effectively replaced the separate subjects of geography, history, and civics in the majority of primary curricula by the mid-1920s.

During the 1920s and 1930s progressive educators led a national curriculum revision movement whose goal was to make the curriculum less academic, more utilitarian, less "subject-centered," and more closely related to the students "interests and experiences." The social studies portion of the curriculum reform was expected to prepare the citizens of the future for lives of interdependence and democratic collectivism. Paul Hanna was the best-known advocate of this social studies curriculum. During the Depression, Hanna argued, children had an obligation to make a contribution to the solution of the great social and economic problems of the nation, not by merely understanding them, but through their social participation. He was the best proponent of the ideas that were widely shared among progressive educators in the 1930s, and which came to be known as "expanding environments," "widening interests," "expanding horizons," or "expanding communities of men" (the term favored by Hanna). According to Ravitch (1987), the adoption of the "expanding environments" approach in the early grades led to the removal of the historical portion of the social studies curriculum and its replacement with a sociological and economic emphasis on home, school, and community. In teacher training textbooks, this curriculum is often depicted as a series of concentric circles, beginning with the child, her family, her neighborhood, her community, and continuing with her region, her nation, her hemisphere, and, at last, the world. Until recently these texts referred to the expanding environments concept as the dominant curriculum sequence in social studies. Little mention is made of the origins or theoretical bases of the concept. Welton and Mallan (1988) were among the first to critique "expanding horizons" as an example of adult logic. The 1991 editions of both the Ellis and Maxim teacher training texts challenge the superiority of this approach and offer alternatives based on recent research and reports.

The psychological claims regarding the "expanding horizons" approach have never been formally tested. Such well-known theorists as Joseph Adelson, Jerome Bruner, and philosopher Philip Phenix, were reported by Crabtree (1989) to oppose the foundations upon which "expanding horizons" is built. In *The Uses of Enchantment*, Bruno Bettelheim challenged the premises, contending that classic folktales, fairy tales, and hero stories help children live better with their existential anxieties and dilemmas. He believed such stories help them gain a surer and more confident sense of themselves by enabling them to identify with heroes who have struggled against life's difficulties and emerged victorious. These examples would seem to support the statement by Ravitch, in a 1989 essay, that the social studies curriculum did not attract sustained criticism until the late 1980s. In fact, the opinions did not come to public prominence until Ravitch, a member of the Bradley Commission, sought them through personal correspondence.

The Bradley Commission recommended three possible approaches to a history-centered social studies curriculum. Each of the models is based on the following premises: that young elementary school children are capable of a progression of temporal and historical concepts over ages and much more complex reasoning than earlier researchers had suggested, that children know more about time and history than has been thought, and that they are capable of more mature thinking when they possess adequate background knowledge.

The first model differentiates between the approach used in kindergarten through grade two and that applied in later grades. The youngest students are to use a "here-there-then" approach, beginning with content from the child's immediate present, and moving outward in space and back in time to enrich children's geographical and historical understandings (Crabtree, 1989). This model is exemplified by the recently adopted *History-Social Science Framework for California Public Schools, Kindergarten through Grade Twelve*. A second model broadens the existing expanding environments approach by including historical and literary studies that connect with the topics studied that year. This approach is exemplified by Van Cleaf and Strickland (1987) in their discussion of kindergarten teachers' use of major historical concepts and artifacts in teaching units about historical events and people.

The third model represents the sharpest break from the concept of "expanding horizons," to a whole-hearted concentration on history, geography, biography, literature, and the arts, together with an early beginning on work with primary sources (Bradley Commission, 1989). It involves yearly instruction in literature and primary documents that are then studied in relation to the historical times they bring to life. Crabtree (1989) considers this to be a child's version of the "Great Books" approach to curriculum making, with literature used to take children into adventurous excursions through historical periods. It is the model which most closely parallels the British primary school model of historical study, and is exemplified by the work of Downey, Levstik, and others, in the United States.

The Bradley Commission has promulgated suggestions related to the methodology for, and the strategies of, teaching history. Reed's (1989) essay begins with a statement which underscores the "equal importance of worthy subject matter on the one hand and effective teaching methods on the other." Reed suggests developing an understanding of the significance of the past through appropriate questioning techniques.

Downey and Levstik (1991) believe that although the current reform movement has drawn attention to the history that children do not know, presumably after instruction, there has been a disturbing lack of attention to what children do know and to how they came to learn what they know. They have drawn the following conclusions based upon the limited body of available research:

> *First,* there is no evidence that delaying instruction in history is developmentally appropriate. Even if mature historical understanding requires formal operations in the Piagetian sense, there is no evidence that the development of historical understanding begins at that stage. More significantly, global-stage theory appears to have limited explanatory power in historical thinking. Research in domain-specific cognition suggests that children know more about time and history than has been thought and that they are capable of more mature thinking when they possess adequate background knowledge. These results argue for an early introduction to historical study rather than delay.
>
> *Second,* the value of a shallow "cultural literacy" approach to concept development in history is brought into serious question by the research. Instead, studies link cognition to context and to a framework of experience rich enough to provide more than surface features of concepts. Sustained study of significant material appears more likely to develop habits of mind relevant to the domain of history and more likely to precipitate the learner's shift from novice to expert thinking.
>
> *Third,* the research on domain-specific cognition indicates that content knowledge is crucial to mature thinking. Teachers need content knowledge to build an appropriate framework

for learning, and students need it to construct adequate schemata and causal theories. But subject-matter expertise is not a sufficient condition for effective teaching. The research literature indicates that content and process count. How one learns influences what one learns.

Fourth, there is an inadequate body of research on instruction in history.

Fifth, the research based on both Piagetian and domain-specific theories has implications for the history curriculum (Downey & Levstik, 1991, p. 407).

History, whether referred to as "my past," or the past of humankind, is the foundation upon which current knowledge is built. Temporal and historical concepts are part of the foundation of the early childhood curriculum, as exemplified by the publications cited on the following pages.

REFERENCES

Akenson, J. E. (1987, Summer). Historical factors in the development of elementary social studies: Focus on the expanding environments. *Theory and Research in Social Education, XV*(3), 155–171.

Blyth, J. (1988). *History 5 to 9.* London, England: Hodder and Stoughton.

———. (1989). *History in primary schools: A practical approach for teachers of 5– to 11–year-old children.* (New ed.). Philadelphia, PA: Open University Press.

———. (1984). *Place and time with children five to nine.* London, England: Croom Helm.

———. (1989, May). Time to rethink. *Child Education* [U.K.] 37–39.

Bradley Commission on History in Schools, The. (1989, November). Building a history curriculum: Guidelines for teaching history in schools. *The History Teacher, 23*(1), 7–35.

———. (Monthly). *History Matters.* [Newsletter]. Westlake, OH: Author.

Burnes, B. (1983, January/February). History for the elementary school child. *The Social Studies, 74*(1), 16–17.

Crabtree, C. (1989, Winter). History is for children. *American Educator: The Professional Journal of the American Federation of Teachers, 13*(4), 34–39.

Downey, M. T. (Guest ed.). (1986, April/May). The children of yesterday. Special section. Teaching the history of childhood. *Social Education, 50*(4), 260–293.

————, & Levstik, L. S. (1991). Teaching and learning history. In J. P. Shaver (Ed.). *Handbook of research on social studies teaching and learning: A project of the National Council for the Social Studies.* (pp. 400–410). New York: Macmillan Publishing Company.

————. (1988, September). Teaching and learning history: The research base. *Social Education, 52*(5), 336–342.

Egan, K. (1982, March). Teaching history to young children. *Phi Delta Kappan, 63*(7), 439–441.

Elkind, D. (1981). Child development and the social science curriculum of the elementary school. *Social Education, 45*(6), 435–437.

Ellis, A. K. (1991). *Teaching and learning elementary social studies.* (4th ed.). Boston: Allyn and Bacon.

Farmer, R. (1983, January/February). The benefits of historical study. *The Social Studies, 74*(1), 14–15.

Federici, J. A. (Ed.). (n.d.) *Yorkshire Tenth to Hamilton: Traveling through time.* Hamilton Square, NJ: Hamilton Township Board of Education.

————. (n.d.) *Yorkshire Tenth to Hamilton: Traveling through time: A teacher's resource guide.* Hamilton Square, NJ: Hamilton Township Board of Education.

Finkelstein, J. M., & Nielsen, L. E. (1985, May/June). Celebrating a centennial: An approach to teaching historical concepts to young children. *The Social Studies, 76*(3), 100–102.

Freeman, E. B., & Levstik, L. (1988, March). Recreating the past: Historical fiction in the social studies curriculum. *The Elementary School Journal, 88*(4), 329–337.

Gagnon, P., & The Bradley Commission on History in Schools. (1989). *Historical literacy: The case for history in American education.* New York: Macmillan Publishing Company.

Galvin, K.E. (1986). Bridging the gap: Strategies for teaching history in elementary classrooms. *The History and Social Science Teacher 22* (1), 43–46.

Goss, T. S. (1986). Using museums in history. In History and the primary school. Special issue number 6. *Greater Manchester Primary Contact.* Manchester, England: Didsbury School of Education, Faculty of Community Studies, Manchester Polytechnic, 86–88.

Gotkin, L. (1967). A calendar curriculum for disadvantaged kindergarten children. *Teachers College Record, LXVIII*(5), 406–417.

Hakim, J. (1990, Fall). A history of us. *American Educator: The Professional Journal of the American Federation of Teachers, 14*(3), 35–40, 42.

Hatcher, B. (1985, July/August). Children's homes and neighborhoods: Untapped treasures from the past. *The Social Studies, 76*(4), 155–159.

———. (Ed.). (1987). *Learning opportunities beyond the school.* Washington, DC: Association for Childhood Education International.

———, & Olsen, M. (1984, September/October). Sidewalk social studies. *Social Education, 48*(6), 473–474, 485.

Helmreich, J.E. (1989, September). The curricular validity of local history: Surface events and underlying values. *Social Education, 53*(5), 310–313.

Hinitz, B. (1987). The social studies. In C. Seefeldt (Ed.)., *The early childhood curriculum: A review of current research.* New York: Teachers College Press.

Knight, P. T. (1989, September). Research on teaching and learning in history—A perspective from afar. *Social Education, 53*(5), 306–309.

LeRiche, L. W. (1987, Summer). The expanding environments sequence in elementary social studies: The origins. *Theory and Research in Social Education, XV*(3), 155–171.

Levstik, L. S. (1983, November/December). A child's approach to history. *The Social Studies, 74*(6) 232–236.

————. (1990, April). *"I prefer success:" Subject specificity in a first grade setting.* Paper presented at the meeting of the American Educational Research Association, Boston, MA.

————, & Pappas, C. C. (1987, Fall). Exploring the development of historical understanding. *Journal of Research and Development in Education, 21*(1), 1–15.

————. (1988, April). *Cognitive change in history: A preliminary study of developmental responses.* Paper presented at the meeting of the American Educational Research Association.

Low-Beer, A. (1986). Imagination and the use of historical fiction. In History and the primary school. Special issue number 6. *Greater Manchester Primary Contact.* Manchester, England: Didsbury School of Education, Faculty of Community Studies, Manchester Polytechnic, 22–25.

Marty, M. (1983, January/February). What do you teach when you teach history? *The Social Studies, 74*(1), 10–13.

Maxim, G. W. (1991). *Social studies and the elementary school child.* (4th ed.). Columbus, OH: Merrill Publishing Company.

McDuffie, W. G. & Whiteman, J. R. (1987). *Intergenerational activities program handbook.* (2nd ed.). Binghamton, NY: Broome County Child Development Council, Inc.

Mehaffy, G. L. (1984, September/October). Oral history in elementary classrooms. *Social Education, 48*(6), 470–472.

Monjo, F. N. (1976, March). The ten bad things about history. *Childhood Education, 52*(5), 257–261.

O'Connell, P. S., & Lavin, P. A. (1986, April/May). A living history museum. *Social Education, 50*(4), 284–287.

Olson, M. W. (1987). Oral history: Leading the way to community-based learning. In Hatcher, B. (Ed.). *Learning opportunities beyond the school.* Washington, DC: Association for Childhood Education International.

Pagano, A. L. (1978). *Social studies in early childhood: An interactionist point of view.* (Bulletin 58). Washington, DC: National Council for the Social Studies.

Peitag, J. (1980). Lawrence Kohlberg, John Dewey, and moral education. *Social Education, 44*(3), 238–242.

Perschbacher, R. (1984, August). An application of reminiscence in an activity setting. *The Gerontologist, 24*(4), 343–345.

Poster, J. B. (1973, August). The birth of the past: Children's perception of historical time. *History Teacher, VI*(4), 587–598.

Preston, R. C., & Herman, W. L., Jr. (1981). *Teaching social studies in the elementary school.* (5th ed.). New York: Holt, Rinehart and Winston.

Ravitch, D. (1989). The plight of history in American schools. In P. Gagnon (Ed.). & The Bradley Commission on History in Schools. *Historical literacy: The case for history in American education.* (pp. 51–68). New York: Macmillan Publishing Company.

———. (1987, Summer). Tot sociology: Or what happened to history in the grade schools. *The American Scholar, 56,* 343–354.

Reed, E. W. (1989). For better elementary teaching: Methods old and new. In P. Gagnon (Ed.). & The Bradley Commission on History in Schools. *Historical literacy: The case for history in American education.* (pp. 302–319). New York: Macmillan Publishing Company.

Richardson, R. (1986). A new look at the educational visit. In History and the primary school. Special issue number 6. *Greater Manchester Primary Contact.* Manchester, England: Didsbury School of Education, Faculty of Community Studies, Manchester Polytechnic, 82–86.

Ross, A. (1986). Children becoming historians: an oral history project in a primary school. In History and the primary school. Special issue number 6. *Greater Manchester Primary Contact.* Manchester, England: Didsbury School of Education, Faculty of Community Studies, Manchester Polytechnic, 36–49.

———. (1986). The place of history in the primary school. In History and the primary school. Special issue number 6. *Greater Manchester Primary Contact.* Manchester, England: Didsbury School of Education, Faculty of Community Studies, Manchester Polytechnic, 5–9.

Sampson, J. (1986). Children as historians: a study of local Victorian families. In History and the primary school. Special issue number 6. *Greater Manchester Primary Contact.* Manchester, England: Didsbury School of Education, Faculty of Community Studies, Manchester Polytechnic, 49–51.

Schug, M. C., & Beery, R. (1987). *Teaching social studies in the elementary school: Issues and practices.* Glenview, IL: Scott, Foresman and Company.

Seefeldt, C. (1975, January). Is today tomorrow? *Young Children, 30*(2).

———. (1989). *Social studies for the preschool-primary child.* (3rd ed.). Columbus, OH: Merrill Publishing Company.

———, & Warman, B. (1990). *Young and old together.* Washington, DC: National Association for the Education of Young Children.

Seldin, T., & Raymond, D. (1981). *Geography and history for the young child.* Provo, UT: Brigham Young University Press. [See: Item # 112]

Slater, J. (1978). Why history? *Trends in Education* (U.K.), *I*, 3–8.

Sunal, C. (1990). *Early childhood social studies.* Columbus, OH: Merrill Publishing Company.

———, & Warash, B. G. (1988, Spring). Buzz saws and bull roarers make history exciting. *Day Care and Early Education, 15*(3), 20–23.

Thornton, S. J. (1987, April). What can children learn from history? *Childhood Education, 63*(4), 247–251.

————, & Vukelich, R. (1988, Winter). Effects of children's understanding of time concepts on historical understanding. *Theory and Research in Social Education*, *XVI*(1), 69–82.

Vancleaf, D. W., & Strickland, E.V. (1987, Spring). Kindergarten children's knowledge of history: Concepts and sources. *Southern Social Studies Quarterly*, *13*(1), 55–66.

Vukelich, R., & Thornton, S. J. (1990, Fall). Children's understanding of historical time: Implications for instruction. *Childhood Education*, *67*(1), 22–25.

Watts, D. G. (1972). *The learning of history*. Boston: Routledge & Kegan Paul.

Welton, D. A., & Mallan, J. T. (1988). *Children and their world: Strategies for teaching social studies*. (3rd ed.). Boston: Houghton Mifflin Company.

West, J. (1978). Young children's awareness of the past. *Trends in Education* (U.K.), *I*, 8–15.

Winks, R. W. (1980, October) In Rogers, V., & Muessig, R. H. Social studies: What is basic? A symposium. *Teacher 98*, 43–44.

Yardley, A. (1973). *Discovering the physical world*. New York: Citation Press.

BIBLIOGRAPHY OF
HISTORY RESEARCH AND RESOURCES

Books, Book Chapters, Pamphlets

301. Blyth, J. (1988). *History 5 to 9*. London, England: Hodder and Stoughton.

This volume on history teaching specifically targets teachers of the youngest elementary school students. It discusses how the study of history fulfills children's need for the past. Chapter Two includes both theoretical and curriculum research. The third and fourth chapters discuss the ways in which young children learn about the past from their senses, pictures, artifacts, buildings, maps and letters, and family and oral history. Teaching and assessment techniques, and resources for learning complete the list of topics addressed. Blyth makes a particular point of including multicultural, anti-racist, and non-sexist resources for teachers and children.

302. ———. (1989). *History in primary schools: A practical approach for teachers of 5– to 11–year-old children*. (New ed.). Philadelphia, PA: Open University Press.

This book provides an in-depth treatment of the subject of history in the elementary school, based on British models. The author discusses the place of history in the primary school curriculum over the years. The chapters on teacher planning and organization, and classroom operation, intersperse theory with practical examples written by classroom teachers. Numerous photographs, charts, and illustrations are carefully placed throughout the text to further enhance the reader's understanding. The extensive, hierarchically organized chapter on sources and resources makes good use of practical contributions from field-based personnel. A meaty chapter on assessment, evaluation, and record keeping forms the basis for discussion in other books by the same author. The bibliography and appendices at the back of the book are useful to all readers as "idea sparkers," as well as to those in Great Britain who have easier access to the materials included.

303. ———. (1984). *Place and time with children five to nine.* London, England: Croom Helm.

This volume in the Croom Helm Teaching 5–13 Series is designed to enhance pre-service and in-service teachers' application of geographic, temporal and historical principles to classroom curriculum. The handbook examines recent literature, research, and practice in British infant (ages five to seven) and junior (elementary) schools. It provides guidelines for the selection and sequencing of content, and approaches to teaching and assessing learning in geography and history. Resources for each subject are described in detail. Part Four: Theory into Practice, consists of detailed descriptions of three units of work actually taught to five to nine year olds. In addition to the references for teachers and children cited at the end of each chapter, the book concludes with a bibliography of items available in Great Britain.

304. Ellis, A. K. (1991). *Teaching and learning elementary social studies.* (4th ed.). Boston: Allyn and Bacon.

See Chapter 5, item 505.

305. Hatcher, B. (Ed.). (1987). *Learning opportunities beyond the school.* Washington, DC: Association for Childhood Education International.

This pamphlet, produced by an organization of educators, consists of articles related to educational opportunities available in the community. Settings such as the library, the zoo, the museum, the workplace and one's own home are discussed. Included are chapters dealing with learning in informal settings, working with computers, oral history, communities with limited resources, working with and taking part in community service groups, and using the family as a resource for learning. Each article includes resources and references.

306. Pagano, A. L. (1978). *Social studies in early childhood: An interactionist point of view*. (Bulletin 58). Washington, D. C.: National Council for the Social Studies.

See Chapter 1, item 106.

307. Seefeldt, C. (1989). *Social studies for the preschool-primary child*. (3rd ed.). Columbus, OH: Merrill Publishing Company.

See Chapter 1, item 111.

Chapter Five presents the child's development of concepts of time and change; the continuity of human life, including the family, intergenerational contacts, and holiday celebrations; and learning about the immediate and distant past. The chapter contains a section on children's use of the methods of the historian. Associated projects, resources, materials for children, and references are included.

308. ———. (Ed.). (1987) *The early childhood curriculum: A review of current research*. New York: Teachers College Press.

See Chapter 1, item 110.

309. Seldin, T., & Raymond, D. (1981). *Geography and history for the young child*. Provo, UT: Brigham Young University Press.

See Chapter 1, item 112.

310. Sunal, C. (1990). *Early childhood social studies*. Columbus, OH: Merrill Publishing Company.

See Chapter 1, item 114.

Chapter 11 discusses the concept of time in relation to centration, reversibility and children's capabilities. The section on history education includes a definition, characteristics, methodology, choosing and introducing a topic to children of different developmental stages, and types of history. Selected resources, activities, and references are included.

311. Watts, D. G. (1972). *The learning of history*. Boston: Routledge & Kegan Paul.

   This slim British volume includes definitions, characteristic features, and developmental theories associated with history and history teaching. As a part of the publisher's Students Library of Education, it was designed to provide an authoritative and up-to-date account of history education for the non-specialist reader. Chapter Four contains a section dealing with infants and juniors, the equivalent of our elementary school students. The final chapter discusses aspects of curriculum and methods, including a section on how their historical stereotypes are "colorful memory aids to children, and are the cues to stored associations."

312. Yardley, A. (1973). *Discovering the physical world*. New York: Citation Press.

   See Chapter 1, item 139.

Conference Proceedings

313. Levstik, L. S., & Pappas, C. C. (1988, April). *Cognitive change in history: A preliminary study of developmental responses*. Paper presented at the meeting of the American Educational Research Association.

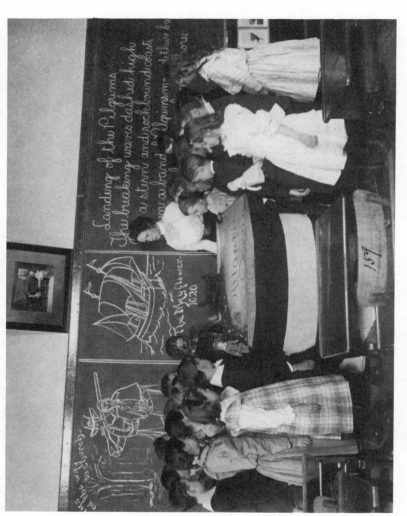

Photo by Frances Benjamin Johnston, 1900. Library of Congress.

Chapter 4
STUDENT TEXTS

During the past ten years, a number of studies on the topic of elementary school social studies textbooks have been undertaken. Very few published studies dealing specifically with social studies in early childhood education, or primary school alone, were found. The primary level was subsumed under the heading of elementary school in most of the research reviewed. It should be noted that two of the three early childhood social studies teacher education textbooks surveyed for this volume (see Chapter 5 for items surveyed), omitted the subject of student textbooks completely, while all of the elementary level teacher education texts included something about the topic. According to Thornton (1991), few issues have created as much controversy among social studies educators as the content of textbooks. He belives that this interest is partly understandable, given the oft-reported dominance of textbooks in social studies instruction.

Historically, the "expanding environments" approach has dominated the field of primary social studies texts. Paul Hanna was a significant force in the articulation of this framework through his development of the 1935 Scott, Foresman textbook series which included such titles as: *Peter's Family*, *New Centerville*, and *Tom and Susan*. According to Akenson (1987), this "bland, conflict free, conceptually limited, middle class view" continued in Hanna's "Basic Social Studies Program," which first appeared in 1954. LeRiche (1987) reported that by the 1960s, educational publishers demanded rigid adherence to the "expanding environments" approach from any social studies curriculum writers seeking publication. Downey and Levstik (1991) state that much of the concern in recent years about how history is taught in the schools has been focused on the role (and assumed domination) of textbooks in history instruction. They cite a 1977 report which concluded that 90% of classroom time involved the use of curricular materials, with two thirds of this time being spent on commercially produced materials, mainly textbooks. Although it appears from some reports that not *all* textbook-dominated curricula are the same and that not *all* social studies curricula are textbook-dominated—for example, curriculum kits, films, and small group work are also used regularly in some classrooms—there are relatively few studies in which researchers have examined *how* and *why* teachers use textbooks to plan (Thornton, 1991).

Schug and Walstad (1991) posit the belief that economics instruction is probably similar to other social studies instruction in the use of printed curricular materials as the basic tools of instruction. They state that although lecture and discussion predominate, teachers reported using other practices such as student reports, library work, role playing, and simulations. Elementary teachers tend to use a wider variety of teaching methods than secondary teachers. Some reasons that most teachers select content from textbooks, cited by Thornton, and by Schug and Walstad, are: practicality, socialization, a belief in the authority of the textbook, teacher belief that students do learn from textbooks, and some teachers having inadequate subject-matter knowledge.

Eisner (1991), provides an excellent rationale for the utilization of many forms other than textbooks, in these passages from the *Handbook of Research on Social Studies Teaching and Learning*:

> The social world, the world with which social studies educators are primarily concerned, is not primarily a world of text. Our lives, and the lives of others are mainly lives of doing and making, ... We want students to develop a critical

consciousness of the society that they now take for granted, often do not see, or believe to be a product of nature. . . . The development of such consciousness is enhanced by helping students experience the world through a variety of forms so that meanings that will not take the impress of a literal text can be developed in other ways. To experience these forms requires that at least two conditions be met. First, it requires that nontext forms be a part of the curriculum provided to students, and, second, that students can "read" the forms that are made available. Thus if students are to have a broad and deep understanding of the pre-Civil War period in the American South, text alone will not do. The music of the slaves, the myths and stories that were a part of their lives, their folksay, programs like "Roots," the music and dance of the period, the architecture of their quarters, and those of their masters, are all relevant sources for enlarging understanding. They are relevant because each tells a different tale, each provides a different kind of content and engenders a different kind of engagement. Text, particularly the text of textbooks, as contrasted with literary history, is often so eviscerated of affect that the feel of the period cannot be experienced. A lifeless text about a difficult and painful period in American history is a kind of lie. In this sense, many of the textbooks provided in school lie. . . . The need to expand the resources through which meaning itself can be broadened is one way to ground or justify the inclusion of the arts in social studies programs. Another justification pertains to matters of educational equity. . . . How many channels are made available for students to tune into? How diversified are the resources teachers provide in class? The provision of an array of forms through which students can come to know and understand a period in history or their own contemporary culture not only contributes to the meanings that they have an opportunity to construct, it contributes to the equitable distribution of opportunities to learn in school (pp. 552–553).

A review of the recent literature, including sixteen teacher education texts, found the following statements, made by one or more authors, regarding the advantages of using textbooks in the elementary social studies classroom:

1. Student textbooks are well organized.
2. Texts provide convenient packaging, because all the needed materials are in one place.
3. The textbook may be used by the teacher as an instructional tool.
4. If one uses the adopt-adapt approach, the text can be modified to conform to local needs.
5. There have been significant changes in textbook treatment of women and minorities. Newer texts portray social diversity. For example, different types of family structures are included.
6. The teacher's guide or teacher's manual is useful, particularly when used as a resource in connection with children's experiences.
7. Useful supplementary materials are provided.
8. Individualized lessons for special needs students and enrichment activities for gifted students are included in the teacher's manual.
9. Curriculum continuity is enhanced by using one series of basal social studies texts throughout a school or district, because a common core of knowledge is threaded through the series.
10. Most primary level texts contain beautiful and realistic illustrations and graphics.
11. Simple explanations and the expanded use of visuals in textbooks can be less difficult for students to comprehend than a complex demonstration or a field trip with many stimuli.
12. Newer primary level texts use conceptual-inquiry approaches.
13. Use of the same text by a class or grade provides a basis for evaluation and comparison of individuals or groups of students.
14. Student textbooks contain up-to-date information collected by scholars.
15. A teacher can find usable ideas in a book, no matter how old the text is.

All sources surveyed agreed that student textbooks are a major resource for, and a central instrument of instruction in, the elementary social studies curriculum. Some authors stated that texts are used less frequently in the primary grades than in the intermediate grades. However, whether the term used was basis, core, mainstay, dominates, primary, or foundation of the curriculum, all contend that the text shapes the curriculum. In fact, two sources (Brophy, 1990; Naylor & Diem, 1987) suggest that textbook content forms a *de facto* national curriculum, usually based on the "expanding communities" approach. Today's student texts are more similar than different in content and approach, because they are designed for a national audience. Publishers try not to offend anyone, especially the major statewide adoption areas, therefore most of them imitate leaders in the field. Elliott, Woodward, and Carter Nagel (1986, September) suggest that published texts often substitute for local and regional curriculum planning and instructional materials development.

Classroom teachers often depend on a social studies textbook, even though it was not intended to become the total curriculum. The book was not designed to be all-inclusive. Although texts cannot fulfill curriculum objectives by themselves, some teachers view the text as providing all the answers. However, it often provides a narrow view, thereby limiting students' social studies experience. This can be the case when the reading material in the text is the only subject matter reading material to which students are exposed. Textbooks have been faulted for having inflexible format. This means text materials cannot be easily adapted to a particular class situation.

Some of the other disadvantages of, and problems in the use of, textbooks in the primary level social studies classroom are the following:

1. Textbooks provide an unrealistic portrayal of women and minorities.
2. Some books are written on reading levels beyond the preschool-primary child. Many textbook series use readability formulas to determine the readability levels within books for each grade. This practice has proved

problematic in the past. A book may be too hard for a class of children who are on different reading levels to use. For this reason, Larkins, Hawkins, and Gilmore (1987) proposed the abolition of the use of social studies texts in grades one and two.

3. Textbooks are dogmatic, dull, and reinforce passive acceptance of ideas. They are not meaningful to children.

4. Some teachers use the adopted social studies text as nothing more than a reading exercise.

5. Research analyzing ten basal social studies texts showed a greater percentage of factual-recall type questions than higher thinking skill exercises in all the series (Woodward, Elliott, and Carter Nagel, 1986, January).

6. Most texts contain separate skills chapters, although publishers contend that skills development is interspersed throughout each book.

7. Skill strands tend to emphasize map and globe skills, because they are most measurable.

8. The use of a textbook as the primary teaching tool limits teacher performance expectations.

9. Used as surrogate teachers, textbooks inevitably fail (Woodward, Elliott, and Carter Nagel, 1986, January).

10. Lack of continuity is evident within some series, when a collection of separate unrelated topics forms the content of each book.

11. Problems were found with the scope and sequence, as well as the presentation of subject matter, in ten widely used basal social studies series (Woodward, Elliott, and Carter Nagel, 1986, January).

12. Concerns with the content included in textbooks for primary grade children have included: excessive broadness, superficiality, needless redundancy, and lack of care in content choice. Texts have been chided for containing non-informative content, superfluous and aimless information, and biased information.

13. Many textbook series are bland, because they avoid controversial issues, or contain "sanitized content."

14. Textbooks become outdated quickly because they are not updated every year. They fail to keep pace with new knowledge from the social sciences because "new" curriculum approaches are not accepted readily by educational consumers. Examples of this can be found in descriptions of the fate of the "new social studies" materials

developed during the 1960s and 1970s. For example, the *Our Working World* series developed by Lawrence Senesh, was, and continues to be, lauded in the professional literature. It is not currently available for use by schools, however, because it went out of print rather quickly.

15. A 1985 survey of social studies textbooks found study of the United States dominant throughout the series reviewed (Elliott, Carter Nagel, and Woodward, 1985).
16. In many books, instructional text takes second place to picture book design. Some authors have called these texts "children's coffee table books."
17. Sometimes, use of a text is inappropriate for coverage of the topic.
18. The manner in which texts are developed and written by a team of people has been a source of criticism (Elliott and Woodward, 1990).
19. Textbook adoption committees (in state adoption areas) should be opened to the expertise of professional educators, in addition to the lay people who serve on them for altruistic or political reasons.
20. Textbooks are shaped by the market rather than educational considerations, because they are big business.

Poor use of textbooks by teachers, and poor teaching practices, were mentioned by several authors of teacher education texts as reasons for problems with the use of student social studies textbooks in the primary school classroom (Banks, 1990; Maxim, 1991; Schug & Beery, 1987; Welton & Mallon, 1988). Use of the student text as the only reading material provided may be due to lack of experience with non-textbook approaches. The teacher is advised to explore trade books and other suitable literary materials. Lack of creativity and dependence on the teacher's manual may be due to lack of confidence in subject matter knowledge. This practice, called the "recipe approach" by Naylor and Diem (1987), can be alleviated through study of the social sciences, and/or through a personal reading program. The problem of limited coverage of significant content material in the text, leads to the building of teacher resource files. It takes time for a teacher to build such a file, and to collect needed source materials from many places. A textbook may also be used primarily as a teacher resource. The teacher would then be able to modify the content for students with special needs or enrich it for gifted individuals. In school districts where there is either a lack of preparation time or of instructional support services, nondifferentiated utilization of the limited content in most textbooks may continue.

Although the textbook is not meant to be covered by reading it page-for-page, many beginning teachers use this approach. They either have not yet accumulated the resources necessary to go beyond the text, or they feel the text should provide all the necessary information to the students. The authors of student textbooks, according to Jarolimek (1990), assume that teachers will guide children in their use of the book. In districts where reading, language arts, and mathematics are emphasized, social studies may need to be integrated into the curriculum core subjects. If a particular book or series of books constitutes the currently adopted text of the school district or state, there is often little choice but to use it. However, the teacher may use the "adopt-adapt approach" described by Naylor & Diem (1987), to modify the content so that it fits their instructional program, meeting their needs as well as those of their students. If no money has been provided for social studies textbooks for the entire class, in grades kindergarten to three, the teacher can utilize a few copies of a variety of texts, combined with research materials and trade books available in the school or local library. The text is then used as a "jumping off point" for student investigations (Maxim, 1991; Seif, 1977). It is a good idea for students to learn to use multiple data sources, both those provided by the teacher, and those they discover by themselves (Banks, 1990; Ellis, 1991; Jarolimek, 1990; Maxim, 1991; Michaelis, 1988). This situation would also necessitate the use of such techniques as cooperative learning, research and higher-order thinking skills, or other independent group and individualized approaches.

Sometimes the teacher's attitude or approach toward the teaching of social studies needs modification. A plan for the introduction of a text should be written prior to introducing the book to the class at the beginning of the year (Banks, 1990). The teacher is advised to learn creative approaches in the teaching of social studies. These may include use of the text, as well as inquiry activities and creative arts experiences. Children in the kindergarten and primary grades should be involved in meaningful interactions with others and with the environment (Elliott, Woodward & Carter Nagel, 1986, September; Seefeldt, 1989). If a text is used, it should ideally be selected *after* unit goals, objectives, and main ideas to be covered during the year have been decided upon by the teacher or teaching team. The substitution of commercial social studies text manuals for this type of planning and instructional materials development is a misuse of these guides. School, district, or state curriculum guides should be relied upon by the teacher during the social studies curriculum planning process.

AN ANALYSIS OF
SELECTED STUDENT TEXTS

Selected textbooks from five elementary school social studies series currently used in kindergarten and primary level classrooms in the United States were reviewed by the author. In addition, a handful of supplementary texts and activity books were considered. Criteria taken from published studies of elementary school texts in general, as well as criteria regarding elementary social studies texts in particular, have been included in the assessment. The criteria and definitions developed by Larkins, Hawkins and Gilmore (1987) [see Table 4.1], Brophy (1990) [see table 4.2], and Beck and McKeown (1991), have been adapted for analysis of the selected kindergarten and primary programs in this chapter. The review of the five kindergarten programs from these series incorporates criteria specifically related to early childhood education practices, taken from the National Association for the Education of Young Children (NAEYC) publication, *Developmentally Appropriate Practice* (DAP), edited by S. Bredekamp (1987).

A glance at the content of the kindergarten level program of five major publishers [see Table 4.3] shows that each includes the topics of families, community workers, rules, seasons, special days, and special people. Four of the five include the topic of feelings. Four include friends. Three of the five include school, and three discuss maps and globes.

The Heath kindergarten program emphasizes projects, activities, and hands-on exploration. It addresses components 6, 7, 9, 10, 11, 12 of DAP. [See Table 4.4]. For example, posters include different kinds of houses; divorce and job changes are discussed; a worksheet depicts the changes in the life of one family. Multicultural aspects are incorporated into a study of the new year celebrations of several cultures that take place at different times of the calendar year. Geography is included in the activities of several units—for example, students placing their house at their address on a large floor map, a poster travel game, and a transportation mural depicting a variety of natural and human created formations. Economic concepts such as meeting needs and using money are taught through activities and classroom interest centers.

Houghton Mifflin infuses historical concepts throughout the kindergarten year. Each unit begins with a poster showing life today and ends with a separate poster depicting life long ago. One poster depicts two types of stores, allowing students to make comparisons. Multicultural, economic and geographic concepts are integrated into the program. For example, holidays around the world are studied through children's books and making items used in celebrations. The class is encouraged to create its own celebration for "Favorite Animal Day." The travel unit includes a literature selection depicting a trip to town taken by Jafta, a Black boy from

Table 4.1

CRITERIA FOR ANALYSIS OF STUDENT TEXTS

adapted from: Larkins, Hawkins & Gilmore (1987)

Noninformative content:

1. *Needlessly redundant*—knowledge that children already possess.

2. *Superfluous information*—knowledge that children will acquire without instruction.

3. *Superficial information*—knowledge that texts treat vacuously. Text information is sketchy, abstract, bland and boring. Authors hop from topic to topic, fleshing only the bare bones of an idea before the children's eyes. When the authors decide to present a more detailed narrative, the topic chosen is often trivial. Important topics are dismissed with a handful of colorless words.

4. *Text inappropriate*—may be important or useful but may not belong in texts.

5. *Sanitized information*—content which has been purged of any opportunity to give offense, nothing controversial.

6. *Biased information*—knowledge which presents a single viewpoint when multiple viewpoints are appropriate.

7. *Aimless information*—knowledge which is not clearly related to important goals of social studies. Content which bears no clear relationship to any other content in the text.

Table 4.2

CRITERIA FOR CONTENT SELECTION, AND EXPLICATION

Brophy (1990)

B. 1. Given the goals of the curriculum, is the selection of content coherent and appropriate? Is there coherence across units and grade levels?
2. What is communicated about the nature of the discipline from which the school subject originated?
   a. How does content selection represent the substance and nature of the discipline?
   b. Is content selection faithful to the disciplines from which the content is drawn?
3. To what extent were life applications used as a criterion for content selection and treatment?
5. Does content selection reflect consideration for student interests, attitudes, and dispositions to learn?

D. 1. Is topic treatment appropriate?
   a. Is content presentation clear?
   b. If content is simplified for young students, does it retain validity?
   c. How successfully is the content explicated in relation to students' prior knowledge, experience, and interest? Are assumptions accurate?
   d. When appropriate, is there an emphasis on surfacing, challenging, and correcting misconceptions?
2. Is the content treated with sufficient depth to promote conceptual understanding of key ideas?
4. Are effective representations used to help students relate content to current knowledge and experience?
   a. When appropriate, are concepts represented in multiple ways?
   c. Are representations likely to foster higher level thinking about the content?
7. When skills are included, are they used to extend understanding of the content or just added on? To what extent is skills instruction embedded within holistic application opportunities rather than isolated as practice of individual skills?

Table 4.2 (cont.)

CRITERIA FOR ANALYSIS OF
TEACHER GUIDES AND MANUALS

Brophy (1990)

H. 1a. Do suggestions to the teacher flow from a coherent and manageable model of teaching and learning the subject matter?

1b. If so, to what extent does the model foster higher order thinking?

2. To what extent does the curriculum come with an adequate rationale, scope and sequence chart, and introductory section that provide clear and sufficiently detailed information about what the program is designed to accomplish and how it has been designed to do so?

3. Does the combination of student text, advice and resources in teacher's manual, and additional materials constitute a total package sufficient to enable teachers to implement a reasonably good program? If not, what else is needed?

   a. Do the materials provide the teacher with specific information about students' prior knowledge (or ways to determine prior knowledge) and likely responses to instruction, questions, activities, and assignments? Does the teacher's manual provide guidance about ways to elaborate or follow up on text material and develop understanding?

   b. To what extent does the teacher's manual give guidance concerning kinds of sustained teacher-student discourse surrounding assignments and activities?

   c. What guidance is given to teachers regarding how to structure activities and scaffold student progress during work on assignments, and how to provide feedback following completion?

   d. What kind of guidance is given to the teacher about grading or credit for participation in classroom discourse, work on assignments, or performance on tests? About other evaluation techniques?

   e. Are suggested materials accessible to the teacher?

4. What content and pedagogical knowledge is required for the teacher to use this curriculum effectively?

South Africa. Economic concepts studied include needs, wants, and going into business. A store interest center in the classroom provides for dramatic play in the economic world. The "Building a Community" poster serves as motivation for construction of a city from boxes and other creative materials. In the transportation unit, children are engaged in problem solving to help travelers overcome difficulties in getting people or things from one place to another. This teacher's manual appears to address all parts of DAP, as listed in Table 4.4.

The Macmillan kindergarten program includes the economic concepts of needs, wants, and making choices. Hands-on activities are suggested for these topics. Problem solving skills are utilized in a discussion of jobs which need to be done in the home, for example cleaning the dirty dishes shown on the poster. Geographic concepts are included in several units. A developmentally appropriate lesson incorporates making land formations in Montessori-type geography pans as a small group activity. However, the "K-Cling" shapes used on a U.S. map might better be replaced by a puzzle map of the United States. Feeling the land masses on the Montessori sandpaper globe, or handling any globe is more appropriate for a young child than using the "text inappropriate" poster of a globe showing land and water. Both the teacher's manual and the posters do an excellent job of integrating children with handicapping conditions and people of different ages naturally into the ongoing program. However, some of the units contain superfluous, superficial and/or aimless information. This progam provides home activity sheets in both English and Spanish, cognizant of the fact that Spanish is the first language of some children's families.

The Silver Burdett and Ginn kindergarten program contains superfluous and text inappropriate content. For example, posters of children lined up to play a game at field day and celebrating a birthday are representations of

Table 4.3

CONTENT OF SELECTED KINDERGARTEN TEXT OR TEACHER'S MANUAL

Publishers				
Heath (1)	Houghton Mifflin (2)	Macmillan (3)	Scott Foresman (4)	Silver Burdett and Ginn (5)
Titles				
Starting Out	*The World I See*	*All Around Me*	*My World*	*My World and Me*
Content				
Me	Me	Me	Me	School
Colors	Friends	Feelings	Friends	Working/
Shapes	Alike and	Change	Sharing	Playing
Senses	Different	Senses	Feelings	Together
Feelings	School	School	Families	People
Change	Jobs	Jobs	Needs	Me
Families	We Are a	I Make	Food	Friends
Homes	Team	Choices	Clothing	Senses
Needs	Rules	Families	Shelter	Feelings
Jobs	Change	Rules	Jobs	Rules
Play	Families	Jobs	We Make	Health
Neighbor-	Homes	Fun	Choices	Families
hood	Jobs	Needs	Rules	Work
Community	Play	Wants	Change	Play
Rules	Neighbor-	School	Money	Needs
Workers	hood	Day	Community	Food
Trans-	Community	Workers	Helpers	Clothing
portation	Workers	Maps	Geography	Shelter
Communi-	Trans-	Rules	Places Built	Community
cation	portation	Home	by People	Workers
Money	Communi-	Neighbor-	Weather	Change
Farm to	cation	hood	Seasons	The Earth
Table	Long Ago	Workers	Our	Farm
Weather	Weather	Transpor-	Country	City
Seasons	Seasons	tation	World	Globe
Special	Special	Friends	Aspects	Seasons
Days	Days	Alike and	Special	Special
People	World	Different	Days	Days
	Aspects	Globe	People	People
	Maps	Seasons		
		Special		
		Days		
		People		

Table 4.3 (cont.)

(1) Gauvin, K.S., & Reque, B.R. (1987) *Starting out: Teacher's edition. Heath Social Studies.* Lexington, MA: D.C. Heath and Company.

(2) Armento, B.J., Nash, G.B., Salter, C.L., & Wixson, K.K. (1991). *The world I see. Houghton Mifflin Social Studies.* Boston: Houghton Mifflin Company.

(3) Beyer, B.K., Craven, J., McFarland, M.A., & Parker, W.C. (1990). *All around me. The world around us: Macmillan Social Studies.* New York: Macmillan Publishing Company.

(4) Schreiber, J. (1988). *My world. Scott Foresman Social Studies.* Glenview, IL: Scott Foresman and Company.

(5) Hubard, J., McGowan, C., & Spees Ousley, J. (1989). *My world and me: Teacher manual. Silver Burdett & Ginn Social Studies.* Morristown, NJ: Silver Burdett & Ginn, Inc.

Table 4.4

COMPONENTS OF APPROPRIATE PRACTICE
IN PROGRAMS FOR 4- AND 5-YEAR-OLDS AND
IN PROGRAMS FOR THE PRIMARY GRADES

adapted from: *Developmentally Appropriate Practice*
Bredekamp (Editor) (1987)

Curriculum goals:

1. Develop children's knowledge and skills in physical, social, emotional, intellectual areas.
2. Help children learn how to learn.
3. Develop children's self-esteem, sense of competence, positive feelings toward learning.
4. Each child is viewed as unique. Curriculum and instruction are responsive to individual differences. Different levels of ability, development, and learning styles are expected, accepted.
5. Children are allowed to move at their own pace.

Integrated curriculum:

6. Social studies themes are identified as the focus of work for extended periods of time.
7. Social studies concepts are learned through a variety of projects and playful activities involving independent research in library books; excursions and interviewing visitors; discussions; the relevant use of language and reading skills; and opportunities to develop social skills such as planning, sharing, taking turns, and working in committees.
8. The classroom is treated as a laboratory of social relations where children explore values and learn rules of social living and respect for individual differences through experience.
9. Relevant art, music, dance, drama, woodworking, and games are incorporated in social studies.
10. Multicultural and nonsexist activities and materials are provided to enrich the lives of all children with respectful acceptance and appreciation of differences and similarities.

Table 4.4 (cont.)

Teaching strategies:

11. Curriculum is integrated so children's learning occurs primarily through projects, learning centers and playful activities that:
    A. reflect children's suggestions
    B. reflect current interests of children
    C. contain objects children can manipulate, experiment with
    D. are changed frequently so children have new things to do

12. Teachers use planning time to prepare the environment so children can learn through active involvement with:
    A. each other
    B. adults
    C. older children serving as informal tutors

    Many learning centers are available.

13. The program includes frequent outings and visits from resource people.

14. Children have many daily opportunities to develop social skills of helping, cooperating, negotiating, talking with person to solve interpersonal problems.

15. Individuals or small groups are expected to work and play cooperatively or alone in learning centers, and on projects that they either select or are guided to by the teacher.

16. Positive guidance techniques are used. Children are involved in establishing rules for social living, problem solving of misbehavior.

17. Teacher limits or contains overexposure to stimulation such as exciting, frightening, disturbing real or fantasy events (including holidays, TV programs, films, overwhelming museum exhibits, depictions of disasters). Teacher recognizes signs of overstimulation, uses prevention strategies to prevent associated behaviors rather than punishing children. Teacher provides an alternate calming activity.

Integrated curriculum:

18. Developmental assessment of children's progress is used to plan curriculum, identify children with special needs, communicate with parents, evaluate the program's effectiveness.

Table 4.4 (cont.)

19. Children are encouraged to evaluate their own work, determine where improvement is needed. Children are helped to understand and correct their errors. Errors are viewed as a natural and necessary part of learning.

20. Teacher accepts the fact that there is often more than one correct answer.

21. Some work is corrected in small groups where children take turns giving feedback to each other and correcting their own papers.

22. Teachers analyze children's errors and use information obtained for planning purposes.

23. No letter or numerical grades are given during the primary years, because they are considered inadequate reflections of children's ongoing learning.

24. Each child's progress is assessed primarily through observation, recorded at regular intervals, and reported to parents in narrative form.

25. A child is compared to his or her own previous performance. Parents are given general information about how the child compares to standardized national averages.

activities that could be done or dramatized. The superficial
information category is represented by a poster showing a
woman measuring a boy's height. The accompanying
questions require short, low level answers, and do not
encourage higher order thinking. In fact, the answers to the
question, "How might knowing one's height be useful in
everyday life?" "(It might help in finding clothes of the right
size; it might be a requirement for deciding whether or not a
person can join a sports team)," are inappropriate and
possibly biased. The poster of "The Earth" depicts children
using a globe. However, although the accompanying text
suggests that the children find round objects in the classroom,
it does not suggest that a real globe be among them. The
enrichment activities suggest displaying a world map and a
globe and asking which is shaped more like the earth. Again,
higher level questions would foster more discussion.
Additionally, the comments above related to the Montessori
globe set are equally appropriate here. The story in this
lesson is text inappropiate. Instead of telling a story about
another class doing a lesson, the teacher should be
encouraged to share this lesson with the children, drawing
upon their actual experiences. A modified version of the story
could then be used for follow-up. Although the economic
concept of needs is addressed by good questions, the sample
answers are superficial. A chapter on holidays and special
days is included in the Teacher Manual. Many of the stories
are superficial or sanitized, for example, those dealing with
Columbus, Lincoln, and Washington. The story of Martin
Luther King, however, incorporates the controversial issues of
fair treatment for black people and peaceful ways of working
for freedom in an understandable manner. A test for this
section is inappropriate, because each poster should be used
at the time when the holiday actually occurs. Matching the
written name with a symbol on a worksheet does not assess
the child's grasp of the signifcance of the person or holiday,
nor is the activity at the appropriate cognitive level. This

program appears to ignore DAP items 6, 7, 18, 19, 20, 22, 23, 24. Although all the programs surveyed provide some type of worksheets, Scott Foresman is the only program which provides a complete workbook, in addition to worksheets, for the kindergarten level. Geographic, economic, and multicultural concepts are included in the program. For example, the teacher's manual models the integrated development of the concept that "we live on earth." The lesson includes using an actual globe to find land and water, a poster which shows an astronaut's view of the earth, a relevant related story, and a symbolic workpage depiction requiring the student to differentiate between land and water. The economic concepts of needs, wants, and use of money are presented. Students can cut out pictures of money to use in classroom activities and games. A separate section on holidays and famous people is included in the manual. Some of the study prints, lessons, and related activities incorporate multiple viewpoints. The majority of them are not "sanitized," but present controversial information in a developmentally appropriate manner. For example, "Martin Luther King, Jr. worked to change laws that treated black and white people differently." Lincoln, "worked to help make Americans free from slavery." Susan B. Anthony was a Quaker, who, "believed women should have the same rights as men." The discussion of Pocahontas includes the fact that "early settlers thought the Indians were ignorant savages, but eventually settlers found that they had much to learn from the Indians." The Scott Foresman program includes DAP items 6, 7, 8, 9.

Beck and McKeown (1991) suggest that student textbooks should be analyzed in terms of three dimensions: a situation model that is a thoughtful analysis of the situation being presented in the text (in terms of the information a learner would need to construct adequate understanding); extensive examples of the textbooks' presentations of the situation, and a commentary in which the investigator explains why the various textbook treatments have been judged likely to be adequate or inadequate for enabling the learner to understand the situation. The situation model is the set of ideas and their relationships that a researcher believes would constitute student understanding about a specific topic. It can derive either from the researcher's beliefs about what is important in learning a topic or the researcher's interpretation of what students are intended to learn from a textbook presentation. Brophy (1990) developed a set of "framing questions" (see Table 4.2) to critique the curriculum materials supplied to teachers. His analysis focused on grades 1, 2, and 5 of the Silver Burdett & Ginn social studies series. In the following paragraphs, the Beck and McKeown and the Brophy criteria have been adapted to focus on the manner in which holiday celebrations are addressed in the second grade textbooks of four current elementary social studies series, as representative of the way in which each series addresses content. (See Table 4.6 for identification of series.)

B. Content selection

B1. All of the series reviewed contain content appropriate for citizen education. Series 1, 2, and 3 attempt to do this by inculcation. The goal of series 3, for example, is to produce the virtuous citizen who is committed to democratic values and feels a responsibility to participate in public affairs. Series 4 focuses on the development of literate citizens who are informed, effective decision makers. Series 1, 3, and 4 include citizenship values as well as skills development.

B2, 2a, 2b. Series 2, 3, and 4 do not appear to integrate or represent the key concepts of the disciplines. They do provide a compendium of factual material, which is usually well organized. Series 1 is the only series reviewed which communicates the nature of the social science disciplines, particularly history, geography, and to some extent, economics. Specific content selected is faithful to the

Table 4.5

CONTENT OF FIRST GRADE TEXT/ ANCILLARY MATERIALS

Publishers			
Houghton Mifflin (1)	Macmillan (2)	Scott Foresman (3)	Silver Burdett and Ginn (4)
Titles			
I Know A Place	*People and Neighborhoods*	*Families and Neighbors*	*Families and Their Needs*
Content			
Literature (in each chapter) Maps Graphs Time Line Globes Grouping Ask Why School Friends Working Together Helping Town and Country Farm Economic Concepts	Maps/Key Floor Plans Lists Charts Pictographs Globe Ordering Grouping Literature Calendar Play Special People You Are Special Families Special Change Rules Do Together	Size Direction Globe Land and Water Everyone is Special Families Helping Friends School Neighborhood Rules/Laws Family School Everyone Needs Wants	Direction Maps Key Pictures Globe Everyone is Special Families What is Change Helping Feelings Do Together Celebrations Where We Learn School What We Learn Helpers Rules

Table 4.5 (cont.)

Publishers			
Houghton Mifflin (1)	Macmillan (2)	Scott Foresman (3)	Silver Burdett and Ginn (4)
Titles			
I Know A Place	*People and Neighborhoods*	*Families and Neighbors*	*Families and Their Needs*
Content			
Neighborhood Constructing Family Seasons Food Earth City and Suburb Community Transportation Trash Factories Workers World Country U.S.A. Pledge Flag Spanish	Needs and Wants People Food Clothes Shelter Love Working For Neighborhood Places Schools Change Country/U.S.A. States Geographic Features Resources History Holidays Symbols	Choices Making Jobs The Earth U.S.A. Maps Symbols Holidays The World Maps Families	Neighborhoods What is Families Better Community Our Country Where is Symbols Leader Places to Visit Celebrations State What is Symbols Capitals Food (Today, Long Ago) Clothes (Today, Long Ago) Uniforms Shelter (Today, Long Ago)

Table 4.5 (cont.)

Publishers			
Houghton Mifflin (1)	Macmillan (2)	Scott Foresman (3)	Silver Burdett and Ginn (4)
Titles			
I Know A Place	*People and Neighborhoods*	*Families and Neighbors*	*Families and Their Needs*
In Text			

Think About Review
  Lesson
  Unit
Information Bank
Atlas
  World
  U.S.A.
Geographic Glossary
Glossary
	Building
	  Skills
	Unit Review
	Atlas
	Dictionary of Geographic Words
	Picture Glossary
	Index
		Skills
		  Workshops
		Review
		  Lesson
		  Unit
		Biographies
		Resource Section
		  Atlas
		  Glossary
		  Index
			Using
			  Skills
			Lesson
			  Reinforcement
			  Evaluation
			Unit Review
			Atlas
			Place Geography
			Dictionary
			Picture Dictionary
			Star Spangled Banner
			Pledge of Allegiance

Table 4.5 (cont.)

Publishers			
Houghton Mifflin (1)	Macmillan (2)	Scott Foresman (3)	Silver Burdett and Ginn (4)
Titles			
I Know A Place	People and Neighborhoods	Families and Neighbors	Families and Their Needs
Ancillary			
Study Guide Tests Home Involvement Booklet Study Prints Posters Map Masters Overhead Transparencies Discovery Journal Professional Handbook Songs Literature Selections Activities Projects Bookshelf	Workbook Activity Masters School Home Posters Tests Maps Wall Outline Overhead Transparencies Music sheets Music tapes Plays Unit Organizer Teacher Exchange Projects Activities Planning Guides Bulletin boards Teacher Options	Worksheets Map Skillsheets Sticker Atlas Desk Maps Posters Overhead Transparencies Teacher Resource 3 ring Binder Classroom Management Tests Charts	Workbook Review Masters Poster Book Tests Desk Maps Wall Maps Overhead Transparencies Teacher Resource File Filmstrips Motivation Station Package

Table 4.5 (cont.)

(1) Armento, B.J., Nash, G.B., Salter, C.L., & Wixson, K.K. (1991). *I know a place. Houghton Mifflin Social Studies.* Boston: Houghton Mifflin Company. [and Teacher's Edition]

(2) Beyer, B. K., Craven, J., McFarland, M.A., & Parker, W.C. (1990). *People and neighborhoods. The world around us: Macmillan Social Studies.* New York: Macmillan Publishing Company. [and Teacher's Edition]

(3) Poole, A.B. (1988). *Families and neighbors. Scott Foresman Social Studies.* Glenview, IL: Scott Foresman and Company. [and Teacher's Annotated Edition]

(4) Harthern, A.T. (1989). *Families and their needs. Silver Burdett & Ginn Social Studies.* Morristown, NJ: Silver Burdett & Ginn, Inc. [and Teacher Edition]

Table 4.6

CONTENT OF SECOND GRADE TEXT/
ANCILLARY MATERIALS

Publishers			
Houghton Mifflin (1)	Macmillan (2)	Scott Foresman (3)	Silver Burdett and Ginn (4)
Titles			
Some People I Know	Neighborhoods and Communities	Neighborhoods and Communities	Communities and Their Needs
Content			
Depending on Others	Living in a Neighbor-	People & Places	Community
Lunch box	hood	Groups	City
Peanuts	People	Neighbors	Suburb
Bananas	Places	Neighbor-	State Flags
Where	Change	hood	Needs
come	Community	Community	Wants
from	Transportation	Celebrations	Income
How grown	Other Lands	American	Services
Jobs	Working	Family	Products
Knowing Your	Together	Earning	Rules & Laws
Family	Grouping	Jobs	Communi-
Ancestors	Alike &	Producer	cation
Immigration	Different	Consumer	Transportation
Alike and	Rules/Laws	Spending	Indians
Different	Choices	Choices	Tribes
Cities	Problem	Depending on	Settlements
Languages	Solving	Each Other	St. Augus-
Traditions	Needs &	Rules & Laws	tine
Native	Wants		Jamestown
Americans	Money		
Sharing	Goods		
Our Country	Services		
Citizen	Taxes		
	Factory		
	Volunteers		

Table 4.6 (cont.)

Publishers			
Houghton Mifflin (1)	Macmillan (2)	Scott Foresman (3)	Silver Burdett and Ginn (4)
Titles			
Some People I Know	Neighborhoods and Communities	Neighborhoods and Communities	Communities and Their Needs
Content (cont.)			
Holidays	Living on the	Community	Customs
President	Earth	Services	Holidays
Voting	Landforms	Past	Columbus
Symbols	Own State	Spanish	Day
Statue of	Natural	Plymouth	Thanks-
Liberty	Resources	Washington	giving
People Who	Past	World	Martin
Have Made a	Places	Colombia	Luther King
Difference	People	Spain	Abraham
Biographies	Indians	Kenya	Lincoln
Helping	Jamestown	Japan	George
Literature &	Plymouth	Maps	Washington
Poetry (in	Pioneers	Globes	Arbor Day
each	Washington,	Land and	Memorial
chapter)	DC	Water	Day
Maps	Holidays	Direction	Flag Day
Graphs	Maps	Biographies	Maps
Time Line	Landform	Calendar	Key
Charts	Globes	Graphs	Landforms
Diagrams	Calendar	Grids	Globes
Globe	Compass Rose	Alphabetical	Seasons
Recipe	Time Lines	Order	Direction
	Charts		Chart (Grid)
	Graphs		Time Line
	Predicting		Sequencing
	Looking at		Compare
	Pictures		Classify
	Diagrams		Graphs
	Literature		
	Play (on flag)		
	Biographies		

Table 4.6 (cont.)

Publishers			
Houghton Mifflin (1)	Macmillan (2)	Scott Foresman (3)	Silver Burdett and Ginn (4)
Titles			
Some People I Know	*Neighborhoods and Communities*	*Neighborhoods and Communities*	*Communities and Their Needs*
In Text			
Think Key Words Review 　Lesson 　Unit Information Bank 　Atlas 　　World 　　U.S.A. 　Geographic 　Glossary Glossary Index	Building Skills Unit Review Atlas Dictionary of 　Geographic 　Words Picture 　Glossary Index	Skills 　Workshops Review 　Lesson 　Unit Resource 　Section 　Atlas 　Glossary 　Index	Using Skills Unit Review Atlas Place 　Geography Dictionary Picture 　Dictionary Index

Table 4.6 (cont.)

Publishers			
Houghton Mifflin (1)	Macmillan (2)	Scott Foresman (3)	Silver Burdett and Ginn (4)
Titles			
Some People I Know	Neighborhoods and Communities	Neighborhoods and Communities	Communities and Their Needs
Teacher's Edition			
Unit Organizer Planning Chart Rationale Bulletin Board Literature Selections Pupil Teacher Edition Activities Projects Introduction Unit Overview Bibliography Access Strategy Graphic Overview Reader's Theatre Reteaching Homework	Unit Organizer Theme Objectives Teacher Options Bulletin Boards Bibliography Planning Guide Teacher Exchange Personal Planning Guide Use Unit Opener Geography Themes Reading Citizenship Resources Meet Needs of Individual Background Curriculum Connection Unit Review Projects Annotated Bibliography	Unit Overview Objectives Introduction Related Materials Extending the Lesson Other Areas/ Curriculum Skills Reteaching Enrichment Evaluation	Unit Theme Vocabulary Project Picture Lesson Thinking Activities Skills Motivation Reinforce- ment Evaluation Resource Organizer Activities Gifted Main- streaming Limited English Pacing Guide Poster Workbook Pages Separate Manual Poster Book Review Masters Tests Desk Map Hands-on Materials Floor Puzzles

Table 4.6 (cont.)

Publishers			
Houghton Mifflin (1)	Macmillan (2)	Scott Foresman (3)	Silver Burdett and Ginn (4)
Titles			
Some People I Know	Neighborhoods and Communities	Neighborhoods and Communities	Communities and Their Needs
Ancillary			
Study Guide Tests Home Involvement Booklet Study Prints Posters Map Masters Overhead Transparencies Discovery Journal Professional Handbook Songs Literature Selections Activities Projects Bookshelf	Workbook Activity Masters Posters Tests Maps Wall Outline Overhead Transparencies Music tapes	Worksheets Map Skillsheets Sticker Atlas Desk Maps Posters Overhead Transparencies Teacher Resource Classroom Management Tests Letters Home	Workbook Teacher Resource File Masters Practice Outline Map Test Desk Maps Wall Maps Sound Filmstrips Poster Book Success Express Package

(1) Armento, B.J., Nash, G.B., Salter, C.L., & Wixson, K.K. (1991). *Some people I know. Houghton Mifflin Social Studies.* Boston: Houghton Mifflin Company. [and Teacher's Edition]

(2) Beyer, B.K., Craven, J., McFarland, M.A., & Parker, W.C. (1990). *Neighborhoods and communities. The world around us: Macmillan Social Studies.* New York: Macmillan Publishing Company. [and Teacher's Edition]

(3) Kahney, M. (1988). *Neighborhoods and communities. Scott Foresman Social Studies.* Glenview, IL: Scott Foresman and Company. [and Teacher's Annotated Edition]

(4) Hyder, B.P. & Metzger, M.G. (1990). *Communities and their needs. Silver Burdett & Ginn Social Studies.* Morristown, NJ: Silver Burdett & Ginn, Inc. [and Teacher Edition]
Frazee, B.M. (1988). *Communities and their needs: Teacher manual.* Morristown, NJ: Silver Burdett & Ginn, Inc.

discipline. Original source material in the student text, and related literature selections from the teacher's edition are utilized.

B3. Series 1, 2 and 3 include life applications, while series 4 appears weak in this area. Series 2 and 3 incorporate family celebrations into the discussion of holidays. Series 1 moves from a description of the modern Fourth of July to a synopsis of how the holiday started.

B5. All of the series reviewed reflect consideration for students' interests. The photographs and other graphics are eye catching and summarize material or depict content in an appropriate manner. Series 2 and 3 incorporate family, multicultural and international aspects of holiday celebrations. The literature selections in series 1 reflect a child's point of view of the historical content.

D. Content explication in the text

D1, 1a, 1b, 1c. All of the series present a (sometimes skimpy) parade of facts and "happy talk" (Brophy, 1990, p. 41). In series 1 the facts appear to "hang together" better than in the others. The treatment of July Fourth and Presidents' Day, however, is rather brief. The presentation of content is clear and the content, although simplified, does retain its validity in all series examined. In some series there is a tendency to sanitize the information provided by avoiding controversial issues. All of the series focus on familiar points in the content, and relate the material included to students' prior knowledge and experience. It would be interesting to see how the controversy over the quincentennial of Columbus' voyages is handled by teachers utilizing each of these series (See Koning, 1990; Stanley, 1991).

D1d. The only one of the four series which attempts to bring student misconceptions to the surface so that they may be challenged and corrected is series 1. For example, the captions describing an illustration of the first Thanksgiving feast include the information that seashell scoops were used because the Pilgrims did not have forks and spoons, and that cranberries were eaten, but not pumpkin pies. The literature selection on the Mayflower voyage demonstrates the problems to which children and adults had to adjust on the ship. The related activity suggestion would help a second grade class discover how little space there is when 102 people have a 90 foot living/working area.

D2. Series 3 and 4 opt for providing breadth of content coverage over depth, while series 2 displays neither breadth nor depth in the discussion of holiday celebrations. Series 1 opts for depth over breadth of coverage.

D4, 4a, 4c. Series 2, 3, and 4 utilize pictures, sketches, and photographs within the lessons. Series 2 and 3 incorporate displays of calendar pages in lessons, and series 3 includes a separate skills lesson on using the calendar in this unit. Series 1 incorporates a time line into one lesson, while series 2 and 4 provide for a separate skills lesson about using time lines. Series 1 provides the greatest variety of representations in the lesson on celebrations, including: a labeled sketch-diagram, a bar graph, and a reproduction of a primary source document, in addition to the time line. Series 2, 3, and 4 limit themselves to text plus a visual, usually some type of picture. All of the representations provided in these four series could foster higher level thinking, if the teacher goes beyond the material in the teacher's manual. The series 1 teacher's edition is the only one which asks questions requiring students to analyze the illustrations, and provides guidance in using the original manuscript of the Gettysburg Address with the class.

D7. In series 2, 3, and 4 separate skills sections are provided at the end of each chapter or unit. Tool skills and knowledge development are separated from each other, although the skills topics are linked to the content of the preceding lesson or unit. In series 1 skills are embedded in the lessons and are used to extend and deepen content knowledge. The skills and knowledge curricula are fully integrated in series 1.

H. Directions to the teacher

Comments in this section of the critique relate to materials for grades kindergarten to three, inclusive.

H1. In series 2 and 4 no coherent teaching model is provided and there are no general instructions to the teacher. Both series use a three step lesson plan throughout: prepare, teach, close or motivation, lesson development, reinforcement/evaluation. Lessons within each unit in series 2 are designed to be used together. The level of thinking activities varies from low to higher order in both of these series. Writing content and skills unit tests in series 4 call for some higher order thinking. Series 3 uses a six-step lesson plan: focus, stated purpose, explain and discuss, check comprehension, guided practice, and assess mastery. The authors' premise, as stated in the introductory section, is that proper practice in the use of thinking strategies can help students collect and process information prior to making objective judgments. Suggested thinking skills strategies based on Bloom's Taxonomy of Cognitive Behavior are interspersed throughout the teacher's editions. Although this series does foster higher order thinking skills, low level questions are asked at the beginning of some units in grades two and three. The teaching model in series 1 is presented in the first few pages and amplified in the professional handbook. It uses a three-step lesson plan: introduce, develop, and close. The teacher's edition specifically discusses the thinking curriculum through definition and explanation of the terms metacognition, critical thinking, thinking skills, and thinking processes. The student text features a "scholar's margin" to help students "take charge of their own learning" and monitor their own comprehension; and sections entitled "think about (1,2) [or "understanding" (3–8)] skills" and "concepts" [3–8: "here's how" (procedural knowledge) and here's why (conditional knowledge)]. Examples and non-examples are presented. The section called "you decide" [making decisions] includes a five step sequential skill model. The professional handbook discusses student motivation, their tendency to use thinking skills, and the teacher's modeling use of thinking skills by "thinking out loud." The teacher is guided toward modeling attitudes and dispositions by, for example, demonstrating "learning from mistakes." Student interaction, student models, groups for collaborative learning, prizing questioning and interpreting, and trying many possibilities are recommended, rather than valuing "getting the right answer."

H2. Series 2 and 4 provide skimpy rationale statements. The introductory sections do not inform the teacher about how the program is designed to accomplish what it sets out to do. Little information is provided about intended outcomes in series 2, with the exception of the correlation of standardized tests with unit or chapter objectives. Series 2 provides scope and sequence charts for skills, but not for content. The scope and sequence charts provided by series 4 are not useful to the teacher. Series 3 includes an extensive rationale statement, scope and sequence charts, and introductory sections. The rationale for series 1 is succinctly presented. The introductory section is very clear about what the program is designed to accomplish and how it is planned to accomplish this. The extensive scope and sequence section is explained so that the teacher knows both why it is there, and how to use it. These sections are referred to throughout the teacher's edition, several times in each unit or chapter. Professional handbook pages define, and provide usable information on, how to use the program with all students in the class.

H3. The combination of student text, teacher's manual, and ancillary materials provided by all four series would enable teachers to implement a reasonably good program. However, the integration of the ancillary materials in series 2 is not fully explained. In this series, units focus on a few ideas, which are elaborated upon mainly through factual content rather than application of key ideas or in-depth study.

H3a. The materials in series 2 and 4 do not provide the teacher with specific information about the students' prior knowledge, or how to determine that knowledge. The teacher can use some of the activities in some series 3 lessons to determine prior knowledge, although there is no specific section on how to assess it in each lesson. Nothing is said in series 3 or 4 about students' existing knowledge or possible misconceptions in relation to the questions and answers at the sides of the manual. In series 1, a section on "looking back," in the units and chapters, helps both students and teacher to assess prior knowledge. Access strategies and activities can assist the teacher in determining the prior knowledge of limited English proficiency (LEP) students.

The teacher's manual in series 4 gives likely student responses, based on the text. In series 2, likely responses to questions about the text, worksheets, and tests are provided in the teacher's edition. The series 3 manual does give the likely responses to instruction, questions, activities, assignments. Series 1 provides the most specific information about likely student responses. Answers to review questions in the student text contain the phrase "answers could include," as well as specific answers based on text material; the teacher's edition has answers to self-check questions in the student text; answers to unit/chapter review sections are divided into several parts, including: answers to words/key terms, answers to ideas/exploring concepts, answers to skills, answers to using critical thinking, answers to activities, and answers to preparing for citizenship.

Series 4 provides very little on elaboration or follow-up. The series 3 manual does provide for extending the lessons through skills development, and into other subject areas. Enrichment activities include some to be done with other family members or outside the classroom. A resource bibliography is provided at the beginning of the teacher's manual. In series 2 manuals, the section on meeting individual needs in each lesson, provides activities for reteaching content and extending the lesson. The enrichment activities, invariably labeled challenging, are merely different versions of skill type activities. They do not add depth to the conceptual development, nor do they appear to enrich students' understandings beyond the material which appears in the chapter. The bibliographies provide sources of print and media resources, including computer programs, which could be used by students as well as teacher. The series 1 teacher's edition does provide guidance about elaborating upon or following up text material to develop understanding.

H3b. The teacher's manuals for series 2 and 4 do not discuss or provide guidance concerning sustained teacher-student discourse. Series 3 includes some teacher-student discourse, but it is not extensive. Nothing is included about probing strategies or responsive feedback to stimulate discussion. There is no discussion on how to handle student questions or comments on sensitive subjects. The teacher's manual for series 1 provides extensive guidance in the professional handbook, and throughout each volume, about sustained teacher-student discourse. The professional handbook suggests that the teacher's role is modeling these behaviors, and using collaborative learning techniques where students engage in sustained interactions with each other. The literature sections placed throughout each book have a "read and respond" section, where the teacher reads the selection aloud and then asks questions; and an "extend" section during which students engage in hands-on activities related to the selection and discussion.

H3c. Neither series 3 nor 4 provide guidance regarding how to structure activities or provide feedback on completed assignments. The special section in the grade 3 book of series 2, on making a guidebook to your community, provides extensive guidance to both student and teacher. Lesson and unit objectives tie each unit together. However, this series provides no information on scaffolding student progress or how to provide feedback following completion of an assignment. Terms are used which may not be familiar to all teachers, especially those who are not recent graduates, such as "cooperative learning." Where this term is used in a "unit project" section, there is no reference or definition given, furthermore, the activity explanation does not give a clear picture of the cooperative learning methodology in action, or the techniques to be used with students. Series 1 provides a lot of guidance regarding the structuring of activities, scaffolding of student progress, and how a teacher can provide feedback. Each activity presentation in a unit or chapter is complete with feedback ideas and how to use (what to do with) the products produced, after the lesson. Suggested answers to "try it!" and "apply it!" sections in student texts include criteria for evaluating the responses. These section are labeled "criteria for evaluating" (gr. 1) or "answers."

H3d. Series 2 and 4 do not provide guidance about grading assignments or participation by students in classroom discourse or work on assignments. In series 2 the answers to the unit and chapter tests are provided in a section at the back of the teacher's edition. While writing pages are part of these tests, the guidance given to the teacher consists of a statement that, "student responses will vary," and some brief examples of what a student might write. This leaves the teacher to decide what a correct response might consist of, and to prepare a method of evaluation, as none is suggested by the series materials. No other types of teacher evaluation methods are suggested. Series 2 makes a point of correlating unit and chapter objectives with standardized tests. This might lead one to the assumption that the authors feel that standardized tests are the best means for evaluating social studies concept learning. Series 3 provides evaluation questions, with suggested answers based on the text, at the end of each lesson. The teacher is referred to "Classroom Management," a three-ring binder, for directions on use of worksheets for reteaching and enrichment, and tests. Many suggestions are given throughout series 1 regarding the different types of assessment measures which can be used. Cursory attention is given to paper and pencil tests. The emphasis is on other types of assessment measures. A page in the professional handbook describes a broad range of measures and techniques.

H3e. The suggested materials for all four series are available to the teacher.

H4. The teacher using series 3 or 4 would need to have good subject matter knowledge, as well as knowledge of the purposes and processes of elementary social studies instruction. These series are based on a factual knowledge/values inculcation approach, and stress citizenship education. In order to use series 2, the teacher would need to have good subject matter knowledge, particularly in history and geography, and a knowledge of techniques to be used in social studies instruction. Background information for the teacher about topics in lessons is provided, however it is cursory, and is often written as though the student, and not the teacher, is to use it. The teacher would need to be familiar with current terminology in the field of education. No glossary of educational terms is provided for the teacher. The teacher would need to be familiar with the nature and purposes of social studies instruction. The program in series 2 could be adapted for emphasis on conceptual understanding and higher order applications without too much difficulty. The teacher using series 1 would need an in-depth understanding of the content and its ramifications. New pedagogical terminology is defined in the professional handbook, with suggestions for implementation of techniques. Teachers would need an awareness and understanding of a broad range of teaching, interaction and assessment techniques, as well as the ability to be flexible in order to deal with a broad range of students. The teacher's editions assist the teacher in adapting the material to a varied student population.

This chapter has presented some of the positive and negative aspects concerning the use of textbooks in kindergarten and primary level social studies classrooms. It has cited the necessity for using many types of materials and teaching techniques to reinforce, deepen, and extend textbook learning. Suggestions for teacher use of basal social studies textbooks included planning, personal reading to develop a knowledge base, expression through the creative arts, and development of a resource file.

An in-depth analysis and critique of the kindergarten materials of five social studies series, and the second grade student textbooks and teachers manuals of four basal social studies series currently in use in the United States, utilized criteria developed by experts in the fields of early childhood education, social studies, and research on textbooks. A brief review was done of the grade one and grade three components of four of the series. These analyses found only one series which addressed in a meaningful way the majority of criteria developed by the National Association for the Education of Young Children (Bredekamp, 1987), and by Beck and McKeown (1991), Brophy (1990), and Larkins et al. (1987).

One conclusion which may be drawn from this research is that textbooks, the dominant social studies teaching tool, are currently used in both appropriate and inappropriate ways in kindergarten and the primary grades. An effort must be made to increase the percentage of appropriate usage. The humanities and the creative arts can enhance the primary social studies curriculum. Classroom use of appropriate literature, music, art and dance selections should be widened. Thought should be given to the cognitive aspects of textbook use. Planning and preparation for the development of higher order thinking skills, such as metacognition and critical thinking, would assist in the individualization of the social studies program, leading to reflective, knowledgeable young decision-makers. Cooperative learning activities would help to develop citizenship skills and appreciation for diversity.

Provision of developmentally appropriate social studies materials for each grade level from kindergarten through grade three, and training in their many uses, may lead to a commitment on the part of the nation's educators to dislodge the "de facto national curriculum" (Brophy, 1990; Naylor & Diem, 1987) from our schools. Greater emphasis on primary level materials development, and wider dissemination of appropriate existing materials, will address some of the needs of our youngest students and their teachers. Perhaps this will lead to more published studies dealing with early childhood social studies education which can serve as models for the educators of the future.

REFERENCES

Agostino, V. R., & Barone, W. P. (1985). A decade of change: Elementary social studies texts. *Social Studies Journal, 14*, 20–29.

Akenson, J. E. (1987, Summer). Historical factors in the development of elementary social studies: Focus on the expanding environments. *Theory and Research in Social Education, XV*(3), 155–171.

Allen, S. J. (1989). *Maps, charts, graphs: Neighborhoods.* Cleveland, OH: Modern Curriculum Press, A Division of Simon & Schuster.

———. (1989). *Maps, charts, graphs: The places around me.* Cleveland, OH: Modern Curriculum Press, A Division of Simon & Schuster.

Anderson, J. (1990). *Families and their needs: Workbook teacher edition. Silver Burdett & Ginn Social Studies.* Morristown, NJ: Silver Burdett & Ginn, Inc.

Armento, B. J., Nash, G. B., Salter, C. L., & Wixson, K. K. (1991). *From sea to shining sea. Houghton Mifflin Social Studies.* Boston: Houghton Mifflin Company.

————. (1991). *I know a place. Houghton Mifflin Social Studies.* Boston: Houghton Mifflin Company.

————. (1991). *Some people I know. Houghton Mifflin Social Studies.* Boston: Houghton Mifflin Company.

————. (1991). *The world I see. Houghton Mifflin Social Studies.* Boston: Houghton Mifflin Company.

Banks, J. A. [contributions by Clegg, A. A., Jr.] (1990). *Teaching strategies for the social studies: Inquiry, valuing, and decision-making.* (4th ed.). New York: Longman.

Beck, I. L., & McKeown, M. G. (1991). Substantive and methodological considerations for productive textbook analysis. In J. P. Shaver (Ed.). *Handbook of research on social studies teaching and learning: A project of the National Council for the Social Studies.* (pp. 496–512). New York: Macmillan Publishing Company.

Beyer, B. K., Craven, J., McFarland, M. A., & Parker, W. C. (1990). *All around me. The world around us: Macmillan Social Studies.* New York: Macmillan Publishing Company.

Bredekamp, S. (Ed.). (1987). *Developmentally appropriate practice in early childhood programs serving children from birth through age 8.* Washington, D.C.: National Association for the Education of Young Children.

Brophy, J. (1990). *The de facto national curriculum in elementary social studies: Critique of a representative example.* (Elementary Subjects Center Series No. 17). East Lansing, MI: The Institute for Research on Teaching, Michigan State University.

Cunningham, J.T. (1990). *On the go in New Jersey* (rev. ed.). Andover, New Jersey: Afton Publishing Company.

————. (1983). *On the go in New York.* Andover, New Jersey: Afton Publishing Company.

————. (1987). *On the go in Pennsylvania.* Andover, New Jersey: Afton Publishing Company.

————. (1990). *You, New Jersey and the world.* Andover, New Jersey: Afton Publishing Company.

Downey, M. T., & Levstik, L. S. (1991). Teaching and learning history. In J. P. Shaver (Ed.). *Handbook of research on social studies teaching and learning: A project of the National Council for the Social Studies*. (pp. 400–410). New York: Macmillan Publishing Company.

Eisner, E. W. (1991). Art, music, and literature within social studies. In J. P. Shaver (Ed.). *Handbook of research on social studies teaching and learning: A project of the National Council for the Social Studies*. (pp. 551–558). New York: Macmillan Publishing Company.

Elliott, D. L. (1990). Textbooks and the curriculum in the postwar era, 1950–1980. In Elliott, D. L., & Woodward, A. *Textbooks and schooling in the United States*. (Eighty-ninth yearbook of the National Society for the Study of Education, Part I) (pp. 42–55). Chicago, IL: National Society for the Study of Education.

———, & Woodward, A. (1990). Textbooks, curriculum and school improvement. In Elliott, D. L., & Woodward, A. *Textbooks and schooling in the United States*. (Eighty-ninth yearbook of the National Society for the Study of Education, Part I) (pp. 222–232). Chicago, IL: National Society for the Study of Education.

———, Nagel, K. C., & Woodward, A. (1985, April). Do textbooks belong in elementary social studies? *Educational Leadership*, 42(7), 22–24.

———, Woodward, A., & Nagel, K. C. (1986, September). Does the tail wag the dog in the social studies curriculum? *Momentum*, 46–47, 49.

Ellis, A. K. (1991). *Teaching and learning elementary social studies*. (4th ed.). Boston: Allyn and Bacon.

Foreman, D. I., & Allen, S. J. (1990). *Maps, charts, graphs: Communities*. Cleveland, OH: Modern Curriculum Press, A Division of Simon & Schuster.

———. (1990). *Maps, charts, graphs: States and regions*. Cleveland, OH: Modern Curriculum Press, A Division of Simon & Schuster.

Foshay, A. W. (1990). Textbooks and the curriculum during the progressive era, 1930–1950. In Elliott, D. L., & Woodward, A. *Textbooks and schooling in the United States*. (Eighty-ninth yearbook of the National Society for the Study of Education, Part I) (pp. 23–41). Chicago, IL: National Society for the Study of Education.

Frazee, B. M. (1988). *Teacher manual: Communities and their needs. Silver Burdett & Ginn Social Studies*. Morristown, NJ: Silver Burdett & Ginn, Inc.

———. (1988). *Teacher manual: Families and their needs. Silver Burdett & Ginn Social Studies*. Morristown, NJ: Silver Burdett & Ginn, Inc.

Gauvin, K. S., & Reque, B. R. (1987) *Starting out: Teacher's edition. Heath Social Studies*. Lexington, MA: D. C. Heath and Company.

Grant, C. A., & Grant, G. W. (1981). The multicultural evaluation of some second and third grade textbook readers—A survey analysis. *Journal of Negro Education, 50,* 63–74.

Hathern, A. T. (1990). *Families and their needs: Teacher edition. Silver Burdett & Ginn Social Studies*. Morristown, NJ: Silver Burdett & Ginn, Inc.

Hubard, J., McGowan, C., & Spees Ousley, J. (1989). *My world and me: Teacher manual. Silver Burdett & Ginn Social Studies*. Morristown, NJ: Silver Burdett & Ginn, Inc.

Hyder, B. P., & Garcia Metzger, M. (1990). *Communities and their needs: Teacher edition. Silver Burdett & Ginn Social Studies*. Morristown, NJ: Silver Burdett & Ginn, Inc.

Jarolimek, J. (1990). *Social studies in elementary education*. (8th ed.). New York: Macmillan Publishing Company.

Kahney, M. (1988). *Neighborhoods and communities. Scott Foresman Social Studies*. Glenview, IL: Scott Foresman and Company.

Koning, H. (1990, August 14). Don't celebrate 1492—Mourn it. *The New York Times*, p. A21.

Kracht, J. B., & Wheeler, L. (1988). *Communities near and far. Scott Foresman Social Studies*. Glenview, IL: Scott Foresman and Company.

Larkins, A. G., Hawkins, M. L., & Gilmore, A. (1987, Fall). Trivial and noninformative content of elementary social studies: A review of primary texts in four series. *Theory and Research in Social Education, XV*(4), 299–311.

LeRiche, L. W. (1987, Summer). The expanding environments sequence in elementary social studies: The origins. *Theory and Research in Social Education, XV*(3), 155–171.

Maxim, G. W. (1991). *Social studies and the elementary school child.* (4th ed.). Columbus, OH: Merrill Publishing Company.

Michaelis, J. U. (1988). *Social studies for children: A guide to basic instruction.* (9th ed.). Englewood Cliffs, NJ: Prentice Hall.

Naylor, D. T., & Diem, R. (1987). *Elementary and middle school social studies.* New York: Random House.

Patrick, J. J., & Hawke, S. D. (1982). Curriculum materials. In I. Morrisett (Ed.). *Social studies in the 1980s* (p. 39–50). Washington, DC: Association for Supervision and Curriculum Development.

Poole, A. B. (1988). *Families and neighbors. Scott Foresman Social Studies.* Glenview, IL: Scott Foresman and Company.

Sarappo, A. (1982). [J. T.Cunningham (Ed.)]. *A mapping we will go!.* Andover, New Jersey: Afton Publishing Company.

————. (1990). *You, New Jersey and the world: Annotated teacher's edition and resource guide.* Andover, New Jersey: Afton Publishing Company.

Schreiber, J. (1988). *My world. Scott Foresman Social Studies.* Glenview, IL: Scott Foresman and Company.

Schug, M. C. & Beery, R. (1987). *Teaching social studies in the elementary school: Issues and practices.* Glenview, IL: Scott, Foresman and Company.

———— & Walstad, W. B. (1991). Teaching and learning economics. In J. P. Shaver (Ed.). *Handbook of research on social studies teaching and learning: A project of the National Council for the Social Studies.* (pp. 411–419). New York: Macmillan Publishing Company.

Seif, E. (1977). *Teaching significant social studies in the elementary school*. Chicago: Rand McNally College Publishing Company.

Senesh, L. (1973). *Our working world: Families*. [Student text] (2nd ed.). Chicago, IL: Science Research Associates.

———. (1964). *Our working world: Families at work*. [Student text] Chicago, IL: Science Research Associates.

———. (1973). *Our working world: Families. Scriptbook*. Chicago, IL: Science Research Associates.

———. (1973). *Our working world: Families. Teacher's resource guide*. Chicago, IL: Science Research Associates. (See Item 223.)

Stanley, A. (1991, June 2). The invasion of the Nina, the Pinta and the Santa Maria. *The New York Times*, p. E4.

Thornton, S. J. (1991). Teacher as curricular-instructional gatekeeper in social studies. In J. P. Shaver (Ed.). *Handbook of research on social studies teaching and learning: A project of the National Council for the Social Studies*. (pp. 237–248). New York: Macmillan Publishing Company.

Tyson-Bernstein, H., & Woodward, A. (1986, January). The great textbook machine and prospects for reform. *Social Education*, *50*(1), 41–45.

Welton, D. A., & Mallan, J. T. (1988). *Children and their world: Strategies for teaching social studies*. (3rd ed.). Boston: Houghton Mifflin Company.

Westbury, I. (1990). Textbooks, textbook publishers, and the quality of schooling. In Elliott, D. L., & Woodward, A. *Textbooks and schooling in the United States*. (Eighty-ninth yearbook of the National Society for the Study of Education, Part I) (pp. 1–22). Chicago, IL: National Society for the Study of Education.

Winston, B. J. (1988). *Geography: Our country and our world. Scott Foresman Social Studies*. Glenview, IL: Scott Foresman and Company.

Woodward, A., & Elliott, D. L. (1990). Textbook use and teacher professionalism. In Elliott, D. L., & Woodward, A. *Textbooks and schooling in the United States*. (Eighty-ninth yearbook of the National Society for the Study of Education, Part I) (pp. 178–193). Chicago, IL: National Society for the Study of Education.

————. (1990). Textbooks: Consensus and controversy. In Elliott, D. L., & Woodward, A. *Textbooks and schooling in the United States*. (Eighty-ninth yearbook of the National Society for the Study of Education, Part I) (pp. 146–161). Chicago, IL: National Society for the Study of Education.

————, & Nagel, K. C. (1986, January). Beyond textbooks in elementary social studies. *Social Education, 50*(1), 50–53.

————. (1988). *Textbooks in school and society: An annotated bibliography and guide to research.* New York: Garland Publishing.

Chapter 5

TEACHER TEXTBOOKS

How do teachers learn to teach social studies? The answer is, usually in the same way as their future students will learn, through a combination of lectures, discussions, practical experiences, and reading a textbook. Social studies education textbooks are, therefore, an extremely important part of the educational program of pre-service and in-service teachers. A survey of sixteen current elementary and early childhood level social studies teacher education texts was done by the author. The majority of the books were published after 1988.[1] Only three texts devoted exclusively to early childhood education philosophy, theory, methods, and materials were found. However, eighty-five percent of the elementary level texts surveyed address early childhood or primary education to some degree. Of these elementary level texts, the Maxim book (fourth edition) appears to have most successfully integrated developmentally appropriate practice, as presented in the early education literature. Some books discuss young children's cognitive development versus that of middle grade students in relation to skills levels; others include the primary grades in discussions of elementary level skills development, but do not separate them out. Certain texts separate activities into those appropriate for primary grade students and those for intermediate grade students. Many books integrate discussions of strategies to use in kindergarten through grade three classes throughout the chapters, while others detail

---

[1]Publication dates of texts: 1991—4, 1990—2, 1989—2, 1988—3, prior to 1988—5.

Table 5.1

INCORPORATION OF SPECIFIC SOCIAL SCIENCE AND SOCIAL STUDIES TOPICS IN ALL SURVEYED TEXTS

Topic	% Texts Including Information on Topic	% Texts Including Chapter on Topic
Multi-cultural Global Diversity Anti-racist	93.75	31.25
Non-sexist Sex Equity	37.50	0
Affective Values Moral Development	37.50	6.25
History	75.00	37.50
Geography	87.50	56.25
Economics Consumerism	68.75	25.00
Current Events	68.75	25.00
Citizenship Civics Political Science Government	68.75	18.75

Incorporation of Methodological Topics in All Surveyed Texts

Topic	% Texts Including Information on Topic	% Texts Including Chapter on Topic
Trends in Social Studies Curriculum Models	81.25	12.50
Planning Lesson	87.50	0
Unit	100.00	12.50

specific teaching strategies for younger children in one place, and strategies for those in grades four through eight in another. Some texts emphasize methodology and resources, while others highlight social science subject matter. (See Tables 5.1 and 5.2)

The early childhood texts, by Seefeldt (1989), Sunal (1990) and Walsh (1980), address the subject area from the authors' differing viewpoints of appropriate social studies content for young children, how young children learn, and the ways social studies should be taught to young children. In spite of their differing approaches to the subject, all three authors agree that the social studies form the core of the early childhood curriculum, and the integrated day in the early childhood classroom. Seefeldt, Sunal, and Walsh are united in emphasizing the practical aspects of teaching social studies through concrete activities and personal experiences, in a responsive environment, in order to help children draw relationships and form concepts. All three books emphasize diversity and global and multicultural education.

The Seefeldt text incorporates the philosophies of Progressive educators John Dewey, Lucy Sprague Mitchell, and Caroline Pratt. Piagetian theory is the foundation for discussions of play, time concepts, and values and attitude formation. The current (third) edition devotes entire chapters to concept formation, skills and abilities, and attitudes and values. Among the specific curriculum areas which receive chapter length treatment are: international education, geography, history, and economics. A wide-ranging chapter on resources reviews appropriate early education classroom areas, materials, and media.

The Sunal text focuses on the cognitive developmental approach to learning. The first half of the book is devoted to building a framework for social studies instruction. Included are chapters which provide definitions, characteristics, goals, and models for teaching the social studies to young children. Practical chapters which deal with planning, evaluation, and

Table 5.2

AREAS EMPHASIZED IN
SURVEYED ELEMENTARY LEVEL TEXTS

*(by percentage of space devoted to the topic or
by author statement)**

504—Skills and abilities of students, reflective decision-making, geography, history
505—Democratic processes, children as researchers, interdisciplinary learning
506—Skills and abilities needed by teachers
507—Geography, special populations, planning and evaluation
508—Questioning skills, evaluation
509—History and temporal relations, geography, building professional knowledge and skills
510—Developmental approach, critical thinking, concepts, role of the teacher and alternative teaching styles
511—Guide to basic social studies instruction: skills, abilities, resources needed by teachers
512—Critical thinking and other skills, evaluation, values, instructional resources
513—Citizenship and government, instructional media and resources
514—Role of the teacher, current events, computers, simulations and games
515—Active learning, significant content, humanistic approach
516—Values and moral development, active learning, skills development

* Numbers refer to items in bibliography (pages 146 and 147).

children with special needs conclude this section of the book. The chapters on multicultural education, geography, history, economics, values, and aging and death education serve as examples of the teaching models and approaches discussed in the preceding chapters. Two chapters are devoted to resources. They provide the theoretical bases for item inclusion, review teaching strategies, and list information about specific items.

The theories of Piaget, Bruner, and Montessori form the theoretical bases for the Walsh text. The book contains several chapters which focus on the child, in terms of social development; learning and problem solving; conceptual development; and special needs. Particular emphasis is given to values and moral development. Practical topics to which chapters are devoted include: planning, resources, helping the child to cope with crises, and building cultural awareness.

As can be seen from Tables 5.2 and 5.3, the majority of elementary level teacher education texts include: skills and abilities needed by teachers, resources and instructional media, skills and abilities to be developed by students, and chapters dealing with specific social science and social studies topics. Evans and Brueckner (1990) take a different approach, devoting their entire book to the skills, abilities, methods and materials necessary for appropriate social studies teaching and learning.

The ferment in elementary social studies which has been occurring during the past five years is just beginning to make itself felt in the majority of teacher education textbooks. The Seif (1977) volume is the only surveyed teacher education text from a prior decade which expounded upon the themes now coming to prominence in professional and research literature. Changes in textbooks are closely aligned with developments in the evolution of elementary social studies curriculum. According to an article in the Fall, 1989 issue of *IRT Communication Quarterly*, California's policy and curriculum initiatives, for example, encourage approaches to instruction

Table 5.3

TEACHER EDUCATION TEXTS IN EARLY CHILDHOOD AND ELEMENTARY EDUCATION

Topics	501	502	503	504	505	506	507	508	509	510	511	512	513	514	515	516
Ideas Definitions Trends	M	H		M	M	M+M	M	M	H	M		M	M	M		M
Basic Features	M	H			M	M	M	M			M	M	M	M		M
Social Sciences				M	H	M	M	M	H	M	H	M	M	M		H
Role of Teacher	M				M	M		M		H		M	M	H+	M	M
Curriculum Models/ Scope & Sequence	M	3H		M	H		M	M	M	M	M	M				M
Instructional Approaches	M			M	H	M		M	M	M	M	M				M
Teaching & Learning Strategies	M			M	M	M	M	M	M	M	M	M		M	M	H
Psychology/ Child Development	M	H	H		H	H	M					M	M	M		
Concepts	H			M		M		M		M		M		M	H	M
Content						M								M		
Critical Thinking	M			M			M		M	H+M	H	H	H	M		

Table 5.3 (cont.)

Topics	501	502	503	504	505	506	507	508	509	510	511	512	513	514	515	516
Individualizing Special Populations	H	M	M			M	M	M	M		H		M			H
Group Work				M		M*	H	M		H		M		M		B
Skills & Abilities				H,M	H	M	B	M	M	M	H	H	H	M	H	2H
Planning — Unit	M	H**	M	M	M	M	M	M	H	M	M	M	M	M	M	H
Planning — Lesson	M	H**	M	M	M	M	H	M	M	M	M	M	H	M	M	M
Goals & Objectives	M	B		M	M	M	M	M	M	H	B	M	M	B	B	M
Evaluation/ Assessment	M	M		H	H	M	M	M	M	H	H	H	H	H	M	H
Questioning	H	B		H	H	H**	H	H	H	M	H	M	H	M	M	H
Geography	H	H		H+	H	M	B	H+	H	H	H	M	H+	B		M
History/ Temporal Concepts	H	H		H+	B	M	2H	M+M	2H**	H	H	B	H+	B		M
Economics	M	H		B	H		M	M	M	H	H	B		M		
Citizenship Civics								M		H					H	
Political Science	M			M	H	M			B	B	H	B	H,M	M	H	M
Current Events	M	B		H	H	M			H	M	B		B	H+	M	B
Moral Development/ Values	H	H	H+	H			M	M	H	H	H	M	M	H	H	H+
Affective Development				M					M	B	M	M		M		M
Law Related							B	M	M	M				M	M	M

Table 5.3 (cont.)

Topics	501	502	503	504	505	506	507	508	509	510	511	512	513	514	515	516
Global Diversity	H+M	H+M	H	M	M	M	M,M		M,M	M+M	M	M	H+	M	H	M
Multicultural									M			M				
Sex Equity	B						B									
Children as Researchers						M		M		B					B	B
Instructional Media/ Resources	H	H	M	M	H	M	M	M	B*	H	H	H	2H			H
Computer	C	C		C	C	C	C		C	C	C	C		C(H)		C
Games & Simulations							M		M	M	B	B	M			
Creative Expression		B		M	M	M	M	M,M	H	H	H		H	H	B	M
Appendices	P	N	A	N	A	A,G	Y	Y	A,Q	N	A,Q,E		A,Q,E	A,Q	A(H)	B
Index	NST	NSS	NST	NST	NST	NST	NSS	NSS	NST	NST	NST	NST	NSS	NST	NST	NSS
Bibliography Chapter	Y	Y	Y	Y	Y	Y	Y	Y	Y	EN	Y	Y	Y	Y	N(F)	Y
End of text	N	H	N	N	H	N	N	N	N	N	N	N	N	N	N	N
Instructor Manual	N	N	N	N	Y	Y	Y		Y	Y	Y	Y	Y	Y	N	Y
Addresses ECE Or Primary	Y	Y	Y	Y	Y	Y	Y	N	Y	Y	Y	Y	Y	Y	N/A	Y

Table 5.3 (cont.)

KEY:

H	=	Chapter
M	=	Subject is included but is not an entire chapter
B	=	Very brief mention of subject
Y	=	Yes
N	=	No
C	=	Computers and computer programs are discussed.
C(H)	=	A chapter on computers is included.
P	=	Projects are listed and discussed at end of chapters. N.B. These projects are for pre-service teachers, not children.
A	=	Activities are listed and discussed at end of chapters. N.B. These activities are for pre-service teachers, not children.
A(H)	=	Activities in every chapter N.B. These activities are for pre-service teachers, not children.
E	=	Evaluation and/or teacher competencies included
Q	=	Questions
G	=	Glossary
NST	=	Name and Subject Indices are together
NSS	=	Name and Subject Indices are provided separately
EN	=	Endnotes
N(F)	=	No references at the end of chapters. They are included in footnotes throughout the chapters.
*		This is discussed in each chapter or throughout the book.
**		One half of the chapter is devoted to this.

in which, "knowledge, skills and student understanding are taught in a dynamic and integrated context." However, a California curriculum specialist is quoted as stating that, "it will take at least 15 years to persuade a 'critical mass' of teachers to make a clear commitment to teaching for understanding and thinking." This commitment begins in the college and university classroom with pre-service teacher education courses and textbooks.

The Schug and Beery (1987) text (See Table 5.2 item 514) reflects the popularity of simulations and games, discussion, and values analysis and clarification activities during the 1970s and 1980s, as described by Brophy (1990). The two texts with the most recent publication dates, Ellis (item 505) and Maxim (item 510), address a number of relevant issues. Ellis (1991), highlights "how teachers think about and act on social studies." The development of nonlinear and interdisciplinary thinking by students is encouraged through the use of mind maps or curriculum webs, for example. Recent perspectives taken from such documents as: *First Lessons: A Report on Elementary Education in America*, a U.S. Department of Education publication; the *History-Social Science Framework for the Public Schools* of California; "Social Studies for Young Children: A Position Statement of the National Council for the Social Studies" [NCSS]; and "Social Studies for Early Childhood and Elementary School Children: Preparing for the 21st Century," which appeared in the NCSS journal, *Social Education*, are summarized in Chapter 4 of Ellis. Maxim (1991), cites former Education Secretary Bennett's report, *James Madison Elementary School: A Curriculum for the Elementary School*; the recent reform movements in history, geography, and civics study; efforts to encourage lifelong learning; and the content and process innovations suggested in the National Commission on Social Studies in the School document, *Charting a Course: Social Studies for the 21st Century*, as examples of recent efforts to examine and change the early childhood and elementary social studies curricula. Maxim, too, advocates a thinking skills framework for social studies instruction. Although he agrees with psychologists that it is difficult to gain an understanding of how thinking processes occur, he suggests a concentration on the operations of content acquisition, problem solving, critical thinking, and evaluative thinking.

It is interesting to note, however, that despite the numerous opinions and controversies in the field today, education for responsible citizenship still tops the list of purposes and goals for contemporary elementary social studies curricula. In discussing this phenomenon, Brophy (1990) reports that "most . . . authors of contemporary textbooks on social studies teaching make similar statements, calling for reaffirmation of citizen education (i.e., not training in the social science disciplines or development of personal life adjustment skills) as the primary purpose of school social studies and for a balanced and integrated approach that incorporates the best elements of other approaches (recognizing these as sound ideas when not carried to extremes)."

Of the sixteen books surveyed in this study, only one makes no mention of citizenship education either in the index or the text. Over eighty percent of the surveyed texts discuss citizenship education in the preface or within the first thirty pages of the book. Several refer to the NCSS statements that the primary purpose of social studies is citizenship education (Barr, Barth & Shermis, 1977), and that it derives its goals from the nature of citizenship in a democratic society (NCSS, 1984). Jarolimek (1990) reminds the reader that although the entire school curriculum shares responsibility for citizenship education, historically social studies has occupied a unique role. Three authors highlight the relationship of political science aspects. Seefeldt discusses the meaning of, and methodology used in, teaching political concepts in a developmentally appropriate way to young children. Seif states that a good citizen is one who participates in the political process and thoughtfully considers the issues of the times. Banks (1990), in detailing his thesis that all citizens should participate in the making of civic and public policy, includes citizen action goals and activities throughout the text. Two authors include the development of critical thinking skills as a part of citizenship education.

It would seem from surveying these sixteen teacher education textbooks that preservice teachers are taught as they will teach. Their texts emphasize citizenship education, as do the teacher's editions of their students' textbooks. Both elementary and early childhood education texts focus to some extent on concept and skill development. Philosophical and theoretical changes are just beginning to find their way into teacher education books, in the same way as they are creeping into elementary social studies series, one publisher, one book, or one chapter at a time.

REFERENCES

Barr, R. D., Barth, J. L., & Shermis, S. S. (1977). *Defining the social studies*. Washington, DC: National Council for the Social Studies.

Beck, I. L., & McKeown, M. G. (1991). Substantive and methodological considerations for productive textbook analysis. In J. P. Shaver (Ed.). *Handbook of research on social studies teaching and learning: A project of the National Council for the Social Studies*. (pp. 496–512). New York: Macmillan Publishing Company.

Brophy, J. (1990, March). Teaching social studies for understanding and higher-order applications. *The Elementary School Journal*, *90*(4), 351–417.

California State Board of Education. (1988). *A history-social science framework for the public schools*. Sacramento, CA: Author.

Epstein, T. L. & Evans, R. W. (Eds.). (1990, November/December). Special section: Reactions to *Charting a course: Social studies for the 21st century. Social Education, 54*, 427–446.

National Commission on Social Studies in the Schools. (1989). *Charting a course: Social studies for the 21st century.* Washington, DC: Author.

National Council for the Social Studies Task Force on Scope and Sequence. (1984). In search of a scope and sequence for social studies. *Social Education, 48*, 249–262.

National Council for the Social Studies Task Force on Scope and Sequence. (1989, October). In search of a scope and sequence for social studies. (rev.). *Social Education, 53*(6), 375–408.

National Council for the Social Studies Task Force on Early Childhood/Elementary Social Studies. (1989, January). Social studies for early childhood and elementary school children preparing for the 21st century. *Social Education, 53*(1), 14–23.

Staff. (1989, Fall). California's reform efforts. *IRT Communication Quarterly* [East Lansing, MI: The Institute for Research on Teaching], p. 3.

Stanley, W. B. (1983, November/December). Training teachers to deal with values education: A critical look at social studies methods texts. *The Social Studies, 74*, 242–246.

U.S. Department of Education. (1986). *First lessons: A report on elementary education in America.* Washington, DC: U.S. Government Printing Office.

U.S. Department of Education. (1987). *James Madison Elementary School: A curriculum for elementary school.* Washington, DC: U.S. Government Printing Office.

TEACHER EDUCATION TEXTBOOKS:
A BIBLIOGRAPHY

Early Childhood Level Teacher Education Texts

501. Seefeldt, C. (1989). *Social studies for the preschool- primary child.* (3rd ed.). Columbus, OH: Merrill Publishing Company.

502. Sunal, C. (1990). *Early childhood social studies.* Columbus, OH: Merrill Publishing Company.

503. Walsh, H. M. (1980). *Introducing the young child to the social world.* New York: Macmillan Publishing Company.

Elementary Level Teacher Education Texts

504. Banks, J. A. [contributions by Clegg, A. A., Jr.] (1990). *Teaching strategies for the social studies: Inquiry, valuing, and decision-making.* (4th ed.). New York: Longman.

505. Ellis, A. K. (1991). *Teaching and learning elementary social studies.* (4th ed.). Boston: Allyn and Bacon.

506. Evans, J. M., & Brueckner, M. M. (1990). *Elementary social studies: Teaching for today and tomorrow.* Boston: Allyn and Bacon.

507. Hennings, D. G., Hennings, G., & Banich, S. F. (1989). *Today's elementary social studies.* (2nd ed.). New York: Harper & Row Publishers.

508. Hunkins, F. P., Jeter, J., & Mexey, P. (1982). *Social studies in the elementary schools.* Columbus, OH: Charles E. Merrill Publishing Company.

509. Jarolimek, J. (1990). *Social studies in elementary education.* (8th ed.). New York: Macmillan Publishing Company.

510. Maxim, G. W. (1991). *Social studies and the elementary school child.* (4th ed.). Columbus, OH: Merrill Publishing Company.

511. Michaelis, J. U. (1988). *Social studies for children: A guide to basic instruction.* (9th ed.). Englewood Cliffs, NJ: Prentice Hall.

512. Naylor, D. T., & Diem, R. (1987). *Elementary and middle school social studies.* New York: Random House.

513. Preston, R. C., & Herman, W. L., Jr. (1988). *Teaching social studies in the elementary school.* (5th ed.). New York: Holt, Rinehart and Winston.

514. Schug, M. C. & Beery, R. (1987). *Teaching social studies in the elementary school: Issues and practices.* Glenview, IL: Scott, Foresman and Company.

515. Seif, E. (1977). *Teaching significant social studies in the elementary school.* Chicago: Rand McNally College Publishing Company.

516. Welton, D. A., & Mallan, J. T. (1988). *Children and their world: Strategies for teaching social studies.* (3rd ed.). Boston: Houghton Mifflin Company.

Chapter 6

SUMMARY

Two sets of strong influences have impacted upon the field of early childhood social studies education during the last five years. As is the case with other curriculum areas, both the academic-discipline-related strand and the education-related strand have provided important input. (See Hinitz, 1977, for exposition of these strands in the area of early childhood movement and dance education.)

The first strand comes from the field of social studies education. It includes the work of the Bradley Commission, the recently developed California State Framework for the Social Studies, the work of the National Council for the Social Studies (NCSS) and the National Commission on Social Studies in the Schools. This Commission consisted of members from the NCSS, as well as The American Historical Association, The Carnegie Foundation for the Advancement of Teaching, and The Organization of American Historians. The Commission's (controversial) report, *Charting a Course: Social Studies for the 21st Century*, agrees with other recent publications from the social studies studies field, which state that there should be an academic core curriculum, emphasizing history, geography and literature, at the primary level. Although there are some scholars of social studies education who have found a variety of faults with the report (see *Social Education*, November, December, 1990 and January, 1991), it does represent a highly respected viewpoint in the field. A majority of social studies educators believe that there should be a greater emphasis upon the development of problem solving, critical thinking skills, treating content with sufficient depth to promote conceptual understanding of key ideas, and representing the substance and nature of the social science disciplines, in school curricula. Social studies educators, writing for teachers of young children, promote the acquisition of skills which assist the child in applying content knowledge to life situations, as well those which assist in the derivation of major themes, principles, and key ideas from active involvement in specific participatory activities.

The second strand comes from the field of early childhood education. It includes the publication *Developmentally Appropriate Practice in Early Childhood Programs Serving Children from Birth Through Age 8* and the criteria utilized in validation by the National Academy of Early Childhood Programs, both published by the National Association for the Education of Young Children. The position papers of other organizations, including the Association for Childhood Education International, the National Association of Elementary School Principals, the Southern Association on Children under Six, the National Association of State Boards of Education, and the National Association of Early Childhood Specialists in State Departments of Education, have also had an impact on the second strand.

The most widely accepted position statement regarding appropriate practice in early childhood education is *Developmentally Appropriate Practice in Early Childhood Programs Serving Children from Birth Through Age 8 (DAP)* (Bredekamp, 1987). Although Jipson (1991) has questioned the document from the perspectives of culture, and multiple ways of knowing, in general *DAP* forms the foundation for more recent work, such as the "Guidelines for Appropriate Curriculum Content and Assessment in Programs Serving Children Ages Through 8" (NAEYC & NAECS/SDE, 1991). *DAP* states that four and five year old

> Children develop understanding of concepts about themselves, others, and the world around them through observation, interacting with people and real objects, and seeking solutions

to concrete problems. Learnings about . . . social studies . . . and other content areas are all integrated through meaningful activities such as those when children build with blocks; measure sand, water or ingredients for cooking; observe changes in the environment . . . sing and listen to music from various cultures; and draw, paint, and work with clay.

The discussion of children in the primary grades contains statements such as:

The curriculum is integrated so that children's learning in all traditional areas occurs primarily through projects and learning centers that teachers plan and that reflect children's interests and suggestions. For example, a social studies project such as building and operating a store . . . provides focused opportunities for children to plan, dictate or write their plans, to draw and write about their activity, to discuss what they are doing, to read nonfiction books for needed information, to work cooperatively with other children, to learn facts in a meaningful context, and to enjoy learning. . . . Teachers prepare the environment so children can learn through active involvement . . . Learning materials and activities are concrete, real and relevant to children's lives. Objects children can manipulate and experiment with . . . are readily accessible.
  . . . Social studies themes are identified as the focus of work for extended periods of time. Social studies concepts are learned through . . . independent research in library books, excursions and interviewing visitors; discussions; the relevant use of language . . . and reading skills; and opportunities to develop social skills.
  . . . The classroom is treated as a laboratory of social relations where children explore values and learn rules of social living and respect for individual differences through experience. Relevant art, music, dance, drama, woodworking, and games are incorporated in social studies. (Bredekamp, 1987, pp. 56, 67–71)

Careful examination of the most recent sets of documents from social studies and early childhood education reveal numerous parallels. They state similar views of how young children develop and learn and of children's capabilities at various stages of development. It would seem that each is built upon a similar theoretical base. For example, the following paragraphs taken from documents representing each strand focus on the development of citizenship in a democratic society.

> The long-term goal of American education is not only to help children develop personal integrity and fulfillment but also to enable them to think, reason, and make decisions necessary to participate fully as citizens of a democracy (NAEYC & NAECS/SDE, 1991, p. 27).
>
> If the young people of this nation are to become effective participants in a democratic society, then social studies must be an essential part of the curriculum in the early childhood/elementary years. . . . Knowledge, skills, and attitudes necessary for informed and thoughtful participation in society require a systematically developed program focused on concepts from history and the social sciences. (NCSS, 1989, p. 21)

Both sets of documents reflect an emphasis on projects and other learning experiences which promote children's active involvement in their own learning. Each strand emphasizes the importance of physical, cultural, ethnic, economic, intellectual, and other types of diversity. Each includes problem solving, and in-depth treatment of topics through integration of curriculum areas. Thus the two sets of influences draw together in the development of curricula for children in preschool, kindergarten, and primary level programs in public and non-public institutions. The guidelines for curriculum content in early education programs include the following:

1. The curriculum has an articulated description of its theoretical base that is consistent with prevailing professional opinion and research on how children learn.
2. Curriculum content is designed to achieve long-range goals for children in all domains—social, emotional, cognitive, and physical—and to prepare children to function as fully contributing members of a democratic society.

3. Curriculum addresses the development of knowledge and understanding, processes and skills, dispositions and attitudes.
4. Curriculum addresses a broad range of content that is relevant, engaging, and meaningful to children.
6. ... Curriculum incorporates a wide variety of learning experiences, materials and equipment, and instructional strategies, to accommodate a broad range of children's individual differences . . . .
7. Curriculum respects and supports individual, cultural, and linguistic diversity.
8. The curriculum provides conceptual frameworks for children . . .
10. Curriculum allows for focus on a particular topic or content, while allowing for integration across traditional subject-matter divisions by planning around themes . . .
11. The curriculum content has intellectual integrity; content meets the recognized standards of the relevant subject matter disciplines.
12. The content of the curriculum is worth knowing; respects children's intelligence and does not waste their time.
15. Curriculum emphasizes the development of children's thinking, reasoning, decision-making, and problem-solving abilities.
20. The curriculum is flexible so teachers can adapt to individual children or groups. (NAEYC & NAECS/SDE, 1991, p. 27)

In the concluding paragraphs of this section of the document, the authors ask whether an approved curriculum is meaningful for these children and relevant to their lives.

These may be compared with examples from a listing of the characteristics of a social studies curriculum found in *Charting a course: Social studies for the 21st century*:

2. A complete social studies curriculum provides for *consistent* and *cumulative* learning from *kindergarten through 12th grade*. At each grade level, students should build upon knowledge and skills already learned and should receive preparation for the levels yet to come. Redundant, superficial coverage should be replaced with carefully articulated in-depth studies.

7. Reading, writing, observing, debating, role-play, or simulations, working with statistical data and using appropriate critical thinking skills should be an integral part of social studies instruction. Teaching strategies should help students to become both independent and cooperative learners who develop skills of problem solving, decision making, negotiation and conflict resolution.

8. Learning materials must incorporate a rich mix of written matter, including original sources, literature and expository writing; a variety of audiovisual materials including films, television and interactive media; a collection of items of material culture including artifacts, photographs, census records and historical maps; and computer programs for writing and analyzing social, economic and geographic data. Social studies coursework should teach students to evaluate the reliability of all such sources of information and to be aware of the ways in which various media select, shape, and constrain information.

9. A complete social studies curriculum for students can only be provided through the support of school boards, school administrators and the community.

(Epstein & Evans, 1989, p. 428)

State Departments of Health, Welfare, and Education have input into these programs through their regulatory and supervisory functions. A broad spectrum of local agencies that deal with children, including local school boards, provide additional input. The early childhood social studies curriculum developed and/or used in each center or school is a result of the political and economic impact of these "outside" agencies, as well as the work of program staff and consultants.

The current status of social studies education for young childen is bemoaned by the NCSS task force on early childhood/elementary social studies in these words:

The overall status of social studies in the elementary school still needs improvement. We find teachers who feel unqualified to teach the content of social studies or who interpret them, confining instruction to a narrow focus on socialization skills, or mere recall of facts from history, geography, and civics. We find that the time available for teaching the basic tools and concepts of the social sciences that can contribute to understanding human behavior receives an ever-shrinking slice of the school day. At best, this can provide only superficial treatment of this important learning. . . . Elementary social studies, especially in the primary grades, continue to suffer a decline in emphasis. Average instructional time is approximately 20 minutes per day at the primary level. . . . Goodlad found that at the primary level the social studies curriculum is blurred by lack of common agreement about what is to be taught. A predominant theme appears to be an effort to help students understand themselves and others in the context of family and community. These topics are punctuated by occasional—and often superficial—attention to other cultures. (NCSS, 1989)

The the arts and the humanities can be expected to have an increasing influence on social studies education in general, and on experiences for young children in particular. As Eisner (1991) reminds us, the kindergarten remains a shining example of the progressive curriculum practices of the early 1900s, despite pressures on kindergarten teachers to formalize teaching and learning. Kindergarten students learn through the integrated, hands-on experiences that exemplify the best in early childhood practice. The adoption of a whole-language approach to reading and language arts, and a literature-based approach to social studies (Laughlin & Kardaleff, 1991) by some elementary schools, may produce connected, humanities-based curricula for the primary grades in schools across the United States.

The next five years will probably see some major changes in what is actually occurring in classrooms, as a result of the current ferment in the academic disciplines related to social studies, changes in the prominance of specific theoretical positions in social studies education, the current concerns regarding the use of textbooks in kindergarten and the primary grades, and the series of position statements mentioned above. The early childhood educators of the future, currently being trained in our colleges and universities, are gaining knowledge of newer and older perspectives on both early childhood/child development, and social studies education. They are learning about appropriate methods and materials to be utilized in the classroom implementation of a variety of approaches. The majority of these new teachers also enter the teaching profession with a strong base in an academic discipline, which gives many of them the basic knowledge necessary for the teaching of significant content to children in the age group three to eight years.

This volume has been designed to present current and classic resources and research in the field of early childhood social studies education. Awareness of the foundation provided by the educators and researchers of the past, coupled with practical knowledge of the present taken from current literature, should enable the early childhood educator to support the development of young children now and in the future.

REFERENCES

Bradley Commission on History in Schools, The. (1989, November). Building a history curriculum: Guidelines for teaching history in schools. *The History Teacher, 23*(1), 7–35.

Bredekamp, S. (Ed.). (1987). *Accreditation criteria and procedures of the National Academy of Early Childhood Programs.* Washington, DC: National Association for the Education of Young Children.

————. (Ed.). (1987). *Developmentally appropriate practice in early childhood programs serving children from birth through age 8.* (Expanded edition). Washington, DC: National Association for the Education of Young Children.

California State Department of Education. (1988). *California history-social science framework.* Sacramento, CA: Author.

Eisner, E. W. (1991). Art, music, and literature within social studies. In J. P. Shaver (Ed.). *Handbook of research on social studies teaching and learning: A project of the National Council for the Social Studies.* (pp. 551–558). New York: Macmillan Publishing Company.

Epstein, T. L., & Evans, R. W. (Eds.). (1990, November/December). Special section: Reactions to *Charting a Course: Social Studies for the 21st Century. Social Education, 54* (7), 427–429.

Gagnon, P., & The Bradley Commission on History in Schools. (1989). *Historical literacy: The case for history in American education.* New York: Macmillan Publishing Company.

Goodlad, J. (1984). *A place called school.* New York: McGraw Hill.

Hinitz, B. F. (1977). *The development of creative movement within early childhood education, 1920 to 1970.* Unpublished doctoral dissertation, Temple University, Philadelphia, PA.

Jipson, J. (1991, in press). Developmentally appropriate practice: Culture, curriculum, connections. *Early Education and Development.*

Laughlin, M. K., & Kardaleff, P. P. (1991). *Literature-based social studies: Children's books & activities to enrich the K - 5 curriculum.* Phoenix, AZ: Oryx Press.

National Association for the Education of Young Children and National Association of Early Childhood Specialists in State Departments of Education. (1991, March). Guidelines for appropriate curriculum content and assessment in programs serving children ages 3 through 8. *Young Children, 46*(3), 21–38.

National Association of Elementary School Principals. (1990). *Early childhood education and the elementary school principal.* Alexandria, VA: Author.

———. (1990).*Early childhood education: Standards for quality programs for young children.* Alexandria, VA: Author.

National Association of State Boards of Education. (1988). *Right from the start: The report of the NASBE task force on early childhood education.* Alexandria, VA: Author.

National Commission on Social Studies in the Schools. (1989). *Charting a course: Social studies for the 21st century.* Washington, DC: Author.

National Council for the Social Studies. (1989, January). Social studies for early childhood and elementary school children preparing for the 21st century: A report from the NCSS task force on early childhood/elementary social studies. *Social Education, 53*(1), 14–24.

Patrick, J. J. (1989, November). The Bradley Commission in the context of the 1980s curriculum reform in the social studies. *The History Teacher 23*(1), 37–48.

Shaver, J. P. (Ed.). (1991). *Handbook of research on social studies teaching and learning: A project of the National Council for the Social Studies.* New York: Macmillan Publishing Company.

Southern Association on Children Under Six. (1984, July). Position statement on developmentally appropriate educational experiences for kindergarten. *Dimensions, 12*(4), 25.

———. (1986). Position statement on quality four-year-old programs in public schools. *Dimensions, 14*(3), 28.

INDEX